"Mosley is always very much himself, and it is the absence of any kind of self-protection, or self-creating, which is finally endearing and rather impressive about the way he writes, and the life he is writing about."—*Times Literary Supplement*

"When unmistakably brilliant writing is combined with natural insight, the result is likely to be most impressive. Nicholas Mosley writes realistically, with an admirable craft and surging talent."—*New York Times*

"One of the most compelling writers in the English language." —Joyce Carol Oates

"Mosley is the most serious and brilliant of Britain's novelists of ideas."—*Times* (London)

"Mosley is one of the most interesting and gifted English novelists writing today."—*New Statesman*

TIME
AT
WAR

NICHOLAS

MOSLEY

DALKEY ARCHIVE PRESS
ROCHESTER · MCLEAN · LONDON

Originally published in the United Kingdom by Weidenfeld & Nicolson, 2006
Copyright © 2006 by Nicholas Mosley

First U.S. edition, 2006

Library of Congress Cataloging-in-Publication Data:

Mosley, Nicholas, 1923-
  Time at war / Nicholas Mosley. — 1st U.S. ed.
     p. cm.
  ISBN-13: 978-1-56478-456-8 (alk. paper)
  ISBN-10: 1-56478-456-8 (alk. paper)
  1. Mosley, Nicholas, 1923- 2. Great Britain. Army. London Irish Rifles, 2nd. 3.
World War, 1939-1945—Regimental histories—Great Britain. 4. World War,
1939-1945—Campaigns—Italy. 5. World War, 1939-1945—Personal narratives,
British. 6. Great Britain. Army—Officers—Biography. I. Title.
  D760.L56M68 2006
  940.54'1241092—dc22
  [B]

                                                         2006016855

  Partially funded by a grant from the Illinois Arts Council, a state agency.

Dalkey Archive Press is a nonprofit organization whose mission is
to promote international cultural understanding and provide a forum
for dialogue for the literary arts.

www.dalkeyarchive.com

Printed on permanent/durable acid-free paper, bound in the United States of
America, and distributed throughout North America and Europe.

When I got home from the Second World War in the autumn of 1945 I knew I wanted to be a writer but I did not know how to write about war. The books about the First World War that I had loved and admired had been about endurance amid the horror and senselessness of war. This could be written about unequivocally. But I had come to realise that the war I had been engaged in was not senseless: it had to be fought, though the horror and impression of futility were there. So in what style could one write about something that was both necessary and futile?

In the nineteen eighties I wrote briefly about my participation in war in my books about my father, who spent most of the war as a security risk in jail. But these accounts were in relation to the peculiar situation of my father. It is only recently in my old age that I have felt at ease in writing about my experiences of war.

War is both senseless and necessary, squalid and fulfilling, terrifying and sometimes jolly, This is like life. Humans are at home in war (though they seldom admit this). They feel they know what they have to do.

It is in peace that humans for the most part feel lost: they have to find out what they have to do. For reassurance they find themselves dragged back to conflict and to stories of conflict. But this should be shown as unnecessary by a true story of war.

The Second World War got under way on September 3ʳᵈ 1939 when I was sixteen and staying at my father's house in Derbyshire. I heard the Prime Minister, Mr Chamberlain, announce the declaration of war; then I went out and kicked a football about on the lawn in front of the house. My old Nanny, who was at that time looking after my young brother Michael, leaned out of a window and asked if I had heard the news, and was I not concerned? I said that I did not think the declaration of war meant very much: there was something called the Maginot Line in eastern France that the Germans could not get through, and something called the Siegfried Line in western Germany that the British and French could not get through; so the politicians would just play their war games for a while, and then the whole thing would fizzle out. Surely the politicians were not mad enough for anything else to happen? My old Nanny did not seem to be impressed, and withdrew.

For most of that autumn and winter my forecast seemed to be coming true. Nothing much was happening between Germany and France. Then in May 1940 the German army went round the northern end of the Maginot Line through Belgium and Holland: apparently no one confronting the issue had paid attention to the fact that the Maginot Line did not stretch along the frontier with Belgium. I had not taken into account the possibility that politicians and generals could indeed be so mad.

In June 1940 my father Oswald Mosley, at that time the leader of the British Union of Fascists, was arrested as a security risk and taken to Brixton Prison to be held without charge for an indefinite period under the hurriedly cobbled-up Regulation 18B(1a), which gave the Home Secretary power to detain any member of an organisation whose leaders 'have or have had associations with persons concerned in the government, or sympathetic with the system of government, of any power with which His Majesty is at war.' My father had been touring the country making speeches saying that the war was a grievous mistake and should be stopped: if we left Hitler alone he would attack Russia and leave us alone, which was what he had been saying he wanted to do. At this time I thought that my father was a politician less lunatic than most.

On the night of his arrest my housemaster came into my room at school (at Eton boys had rooms on their own) and told me that he had been telephoned by my stepmother who had asked him to break the news to me of my father's arrest. I thanked him; but he hung about as if there was something more to be said. I could not think what this might be. The he murmured something like – Did I think there was anything to it? I realised he was asking me if I thought my father might be considered a traitor. I said – Oh no, he just thinks this war is a mistake. My housemaster seemed dubious, but left it at that.

I realised that things might be difficult, however, when I went out to attend an early morning class: a frequent anxiety had been what there might be about my father in the papers. But one of the virtues of Eton is, or was, that many boys come from families used to the ways of maverick politicians – some of whom in the past might indeed have spent time in jail on matters of principle. So in the morning there were glances, but not much was said.

It did not strike me that I myself should do anything other than volunteer to join the army when I would be due to be called up on my nineteenth birthday in June 1942. I saw what my father meant about the war being a mistake; but this did not seem to be relevant to me. Most Etonians who had not got family connections with the other services or with cavalry regiments opted to go into one of the Guards regiments; or if they wished to be slightly less conventional, into the Rifle Brigade or the King's Royal Rifle Corps. Myself and my contemporary friends planned to apply to join the Rifle Brigade, in the hope of becoming officers.

There were two grave impediments to my being accepted as a potential officer. The first was my father, who was still in jail, although now in Holloway with my stepmother (after more than a year as ordinary prisoners they had been allowed to share a double cell there at the insistence of Winston Churchill, who had once been a friend of both). But hostility against them in the country was still strong. The second snag was that from the age of about seven I had a bad stammer. Of course some kind of war-work would be available to me – but an infantry officer? Lives might depend on the ability of an officer to give rapid orders.

The difficulty about my father was somewhat balanced by the influence of my formidable aunt, Irene Ravensdale, my dead mother's older sister, and a Baroness in her own right. She was acquainted with the Colonel-in-Chief of the Rifle Brigade: these were the days of the old-boy-net, when people supposedly of influence could be expected to know one another. So my aunt had a word with the Colonel and explained – I have no idea what she explained, but by the time a Rifle Brigade recruiting team came down to Eton to hold interviews with potential officers, I was told that I would be accepted as a trainee, although this did not guarantee that I would graduate.

So in April 1942 I travelled with a group of mostly other ex-public-schoolboys to the Rifle Brigade depot at Winchester, where for three months we were to be treated no differently from other newly recruited ranks. I wrote to my sister of our arrival at Winchester Station –

> At once of course we split up into our school cliques – Etonians rather aloof and bored and hands in pockets: the rest alternating between Rugby raucousness and grammar-school timidity. We walked crocodile-wise, Etonians at least 100 yards in the rear, until we arrived at a place which reminded me of Brixton . . . We were herded to our quarters which were like the basement of a morgue, with rows of beds constructed of steel bars, many vertical, and a few bent horizontal and arranged neatly so that the bars coincided with one's hips and the gaps with one's head and waist.

My sister, two years older than I, was at this time doing war-work in London, making bits and pieces for armaments.

It was the style of Etonians to be flippant or condescending about things that might be unpleasant; thus one had managed to get through much of school life. It did not seem that the army would be very different.

A week or two later I was writing to my father –

> The routine is as intense as expected; non-stop from 6.30 to 6 and very often extra fatigue after that. But there is barely time to stay depressed, and the evenings are made happy by the mere fact that we can get outside the barrack gates. We are all mixed up with the conscripts – men of 35-40 – better than younger ones who might be more aggressively hostile to us future (we hope) officers. But these are bad enough. They fuss around swearing (*always* the same drab monosyllable) spitting and interfering with everyone with hoarse belches of amusement. The sergeants are wonderful men, who give us hell on the parade ground, calling us such names as make us laugh and wonder at their power to conceive such obscenities. Off duty they do quite a lot to help us.

My sister and I had visited my father two or three times when he had been in Brixton prison. We had been under supervision in an austere visiting room and had been amazed at our father's cheerfulness. He said he was making profitable use of his time by being taught German by some of the internees;

and he then hoped to embark on a course of reading European literature and philosophy. It was as if, having made his public protests about the war, he was not outraged that he should be in prison.

At Winchester the ex-public-schoolboys on the whole seemed better than others for instance at having to shave and wash and wash up in cold water; the conscripts were better at the ritual of setting out in meticulous geometrical order their bedding and equipment ready for inspection every morning. What I remember now about the Depot at Winchester is the strange mixture of bonhomie and misery – the former mostly to do with drinking beer in the evenings and making jokes; the latter often to do with my stammer. We potential officers would be taken out of our squad one by one on the parade ground and put in charge of the drill. It sometimes seemed that I, standing with my mouth open silently like an Aunt Sally at a fairground, might unwittingly become like the Emperor Christophe of Haiti who used for his amusement to march his crack troops over a cliff. Once when my squad was proceeding at the fast trot that was the customary style of the Rifle Brigade straight towards the doorway that led from the parade ground to the NAAFI canteen, I thought there might occur some happy outcome to my predicament. But the sergeant-instructor beside me, sensing a plot, bellowed in time 'About turn! Left turn! Right turn! Knees up! At the double!' with appropriate expletives. The insults that the sergeants were accustomed to hurl at us were enjoyable, though they were usually gentle with me. I had a friend called Pollock who became something of the squad butt. When we were standing to attention the sergeant would stand very close to him and yell – 'Pollock! Spell it with a P do you? You sack of shit!'

From Winchester I was given leave to go up to London once a week to see a stammer specialist. This was Dr Lionel Logue, who had been treating the King. I had been going to him during my last year at Eton, and I did not think he was doing me much good. I desperately wanted to get rid of my stammer: but he tried to get me speaking in lilting rhythmical cadences like a ham actor or a politician or a clergyman. While I was with him I could do this quite well; then when I got away it seemed I would rather stammer than sound like a actor or a politician or a clergyman. No one made much sense of my stammer until I was sent by the army after the war to another quite different type of specialist. He said – But has it ever struck you that you may not really want to get rid of your stammer? I was for a moment outraged: me not want to get rid of the stammer that caused me such misery? He explained how a stammer might be a form of self-protection. But the understanding of this belongs to a later part of the story.

Some of our squad had been at school at Winchester just down the hill, and they would go down on Saturdays to visit the boys they had perhaps been in love with at school. Then on Sundays we would line up for Church Parade and march to the stunningly beautiful Winchester Cathedral where one of the popular hymns was to the tune of the German National Anthem, and we would try to remember the German words. Then on our way back through the streets, proudly led by the regimental band playing the Rifle Brigade march, we would sing its time-honoured words –

> Oh the Rifle Brigade has gone away
> And they've left all the girls in the family way
> The KRRs who are coming behind
> Will have seven-and-six a week to find

seven-and-six being the cost in those days of the upkeep of a child.

No one at the Depot seemed much interested in my father; and I was not thinking much about the sense or ethics of the War. It seemed we were all involved in some gigantic juggernaut of fate or the grim workings of evolution. Our task was just to keep going, with as much good humour as possible. By this time both Russia and America were in the war against Hitler, so there was the sense that in the end, so long as one stayed alive, things would turn out all right.

From Winchester our group of mainly ex-public-schoolboys went briefly to Tidworth on Salisbury Plain; here we did training with transport. The speciality of the Rifle Brigade and the King's Royal Rifle Corps was to form motorised battalions ready for quick deployment in war. Then from Tidworth we moved to an Officer Cadet Training Unit in York. Here we were treated more specifically as potential officers: we did tactical training at platoon and company level. But we still had to go regularly on long half-jogging marches covering ten miles in two hours, carrying heavy packs and weapons; we were tested for the dexterity with which we could take various weapons to bits and put them together again. We learned to drive trucks: we were taken on cross-country motorbike rides by a former hill-climbing champion during which he led us up almost vertical slopes and we laughed when our machines tipped over backwards and chased us down the hill. We were lectured on current affairs and regimental history. We also felt free to indulge in some of the more traditional pastimes of officers.

I had asked my father if I could borrow his shotgun. I wrote to him from Fulford Barracks, York –

Many happy returns of the day.

Your lawyer has managed to rescue your guns from the Home Office, and they are now safely up here with me. The trouble is cartridges, which are practically unobtainable, but perhaps some of my sporting-sweat friends in the OCTU will be able to wheedle me some from their family dealers. I will be able to get in a fairly regular shoot on Saturday afternoons, and we are now being encouraged to take a gun when we go on manoeuvres on the moors. The authorities are very reasonable about all this; and if one gives a pheasant or two to the officers' mess they will let you take a gun almost anywhere.

We have now finished out mechanic's course, from which I passed as a 1st class driver-mechanic, which was really very bogus, and was granted only through systematic flattering of the instructor. Also our wireless course, which was not so successful, as I was rather over-confident and idle, spending most of the time listening to the BBC and trying to wreck the wireless schemes by sending false messages. Which displeased people, and I fear I may have got a low mark.

But we are embarking upon the most important part of our training now – endless tactics and toughening courses, horrible 5-day manoeuvres in Northumberland, sleeping open-air with one blanket and being harassed by live ammunition and artillery barrages. Then on December 18 we pass out complete with natty suiting and prominent chest and are allowed to show off to our families for a week or so. I will come and see you then just before Christmas.

The times that it seems meant most to me while I was stationed at York were those when I could get away at weekends to the home of an old school friend, Timmy, some five or six miles away: here a group of us continued enthusiastically to play the games we had played as children – a chasing-and-capture-and-escaping game called Lions; acting games, pencil-and-paper games. Then occasionally at weekends, I and others would be able to get down to London where my sister shared a flat with two girlfriends also working in her small-arms business. We would land up in a favourite nightclub called The Nut House where we drank and sang communal songs like "The Sheik of Araby" (to which the antiphon was *With no pants on); or* "Bell-bottom Trousers Coats of Navy Blue" (antiphon: *He'll climb the rigging like his father used to do).* These chants have stuck in my mind like strange mantras. The lady who ran The Nut House told me she had known my father, and did I know how attractive my stammer was? I said – No. This might have been a life-giving moment for me.

When the time came for I and my colleagues either to become officers or to have failed, I was interviewed by the young captain who had largely been responsible for our training and he told me that they did not usually commission cadets with a stammer as bad as mine; but – but – I don't remember him quite being able to finish this sentence. But anyway there I was, turning up in London for Christmas 1942 resplendent in my new 2nd Lieutenant's uniform. And the Battle of El Alamein had by this time been won, and the battle of Stalingrad was going all right, was it not? And the war seemed as distant as ancient mythology.

One of the consequences of my having become an officer was that I got permission from the Home Office to spend the best part of a day with my father and stepmother in Holloway Jail. So in the New Year I dropped in at Fortnum and Mason on the way and arrived with the inside of my huge army overcoat hung with a ham and a bottle of brandy, and under my arm a Wagner record for Diana's wind-up gramophone with a giant horn. We had a fine day – this was the first time I felt old enough to talk on anything like equal terms with my father – we did not say much about the war: we talked about ideas and books. Then towards the end of the day there was a knock on the door of the bleak cell-like room where my father and stepmother and I were sampling the brandy; my father said 'Who is it?' and a voice said 'The Governor.' My father said 'Oh do come in!' and made a half-hearted attempt to hide the bottle under the table. The Governor was a pleasant man and he stayed and chatted with us for a while, then my father said 'Would you like a glass of brandy?' The Governor said 'Thank you!' My stepmother went off to wash a tooth-glass. The Governor said 'Ah, you don't often find brandy like this nowadays!'

My father still seemed extraordinarily serene in prison; it was as if prison was the evidence of his disapproval of war. Then on a later visit when we were alone together for a while he did speak briefly of the war: he said that when I went abroad to fight, if ever it happened that I were taken prisoner, then I should remember some password that he would give me in case he were able to get in touch with me. I thought this odd: surely my father could have no contacts now with Germany? And he had never, unlike my stepmother, been on close personal terms with high-up Nazis. I thought – This is just a way of implying that he might still have a finger in the world of intrigue. But I did perhaps begin to wonder – Well it might not be such a bad thing after all to be taken prisoner and so survive a war which before long, surely, will be as good as won. But what a time it might still take to finish it off – for armies to slog to and fro across North Africa, and all the way back across Russia to Berlin.

- 2 -

Newly-commissioned officers waiting to be sent overseas went
to the Rifle Brigade Holding Battalion at Ranby, in Notting-
hamshire; a rather bleak encampment of huts either side of the
Retford-Worksop Road. But here everything became different.

We felt ourselves liberated from institutional subservience;
from the need to ingratiate and dissemble. We could begin to be
what we felt we were; but most of us were only nineteen.

We were each to be in charge of the training of a platoon
of thirty to thirty-five men, most of them much older than
ourselves. I wrote to my Aunt Irene –

> At the moment I have a platoon of 35 men all to myself
> who are only just starting their training, and who
> are ignorant and stupid beyond belief. So I have a
> hard and anxious job, but I believe when some of the
> other officers come back off leave I may have someone
> to help me. Unfortunately I was given the platoon
> which had the reputation of being the scruffiest in

the Company, and now it is up to me I suppose to descruff them. They never wash, lose all their equipment and come out half-dressed; but are incredibly keen when out training in the country, and good fun if you treat them right. They are so shabby and slack about their appearance and their barrack room, and yet they are so pleasant and good-natured when one chats to them. I try to be both pleasant and firm, but it is tricky.

The time is taken up with Weapon Training, which I leave to the NCOs, who are efficient, and can do that sort of thing much better than us: unending lectures on Gas, Map Reading, Tactics, and even First Aid and Topical Interest, which I give, rather shakily at first, but I am getting used to it now, and am becoming reasonably good. My sergeant is very helpful. I really do take my hat off to these old NCOs, some of whom have been in the army for years. They all play up to us junior officers, and there is no question of the jealousy which I believe you get in some regiments.

To my old school friend, Timmy, who was following in my footsteps a few months behind me, and who had written asking for hints from which he could learn, I wrote –

So long as you tell your sergeant just what you want done and leave him to do it in his own way, the house on fire burns merrily. It is only when you butt in on the sergeant's pitch, and quibble with him in front of the men, that the trouble starts. When you want to take over the platoon he will step into the background and help without pestering suggestions.

With the men I have so far got on well, and we have been able to laugh together and they do have respect. I have only had to deliver one personal rocket when I saw a man chewing gum on parade. I told him to spit it out, to which he answered that he was unable because it had stuck to the roof of his palate. I then waxed vicious and said that he either got his gum unstuck or I would get him so stuck himself that he would not be able to extricate himself for weeks, at which he accordingly expectorated (is this the word?) and so we went on.

Later. Christ, am I weary this evening. My platoon is really too bloody keen for words. They led me slap through a river today, and I had to follow with pretence of enjoyment. But they are fun, and so much more worthwhile than the old sweats I was with at Winch.

When we went out on manoeuvres we were able to go to the beautiful Peak District of Derbyshire, where it seemed to make sense to do tactical training in the style of stalking-and-catching-and-rescuing games which my friends and I had played ever since childhood. My friend and colleague during these exercises was Raleigh Trevelyan, who later was to write one of the best books about fighting in the Second World War, *The Fortress*, about his experiences at the landing at Anzio. In the Peak District we would pit our platoons against each other like Cowboys and

Indians; in the evenings we would all sit around camp fires and sing songs under the stars. We junior officers often felt more at home with our men than we did in the officer's mess at Ranby. I wrote to my sister –

> I really think that the usual life of an officer is even more narrowing and binding than that of a man. In the ranks one was admittedly restricted physically by petty regulations, but as an officer one is up against the appalling tyranny of etiquette and good manners. The mess is stuffy and staid like a Victorian clubroom; and there is no escape. One cannot even roll out and wallow in a pub. One is always under the eye of a keen and critical audience.

It seems that I was beginning to realise that in describing my men as scruffy and unruly, and yet also in important ways the salt of the earth, there was indeed a tradition in which these were likely to be aspects of the same thing.

And before long we junior officers were creating our own manner of anarchic protest by turning one of our rooms (we had rooms which two of us shared in a large hut on its own) into a fantasy nightclub which we called The Juke Box. Here, away from the Officers' Mess, we played records on a wind-up gramophone; we danced ballroom or exotic dances; some of us got hold of women's clothes. There is a tradition in armies for this sort of thing on the fringes of war – presumably as a reaction or counterbalance to the brutally macho business of killing; perhaps psychologically as a form of bonding. I do not know how many of us were at that time, or remained, in fact gay: there was no evidence at the time of anything overtly sexual. We had nearly all come from public schools where it seemed naturally the fashion to behave in a gay style; what better could one do with no girls in sight? I myself had been no exception to this. The word 'gay' had not been applied to homosexuality yet, but one can see how this use of it arose. Homosexuals were seen as paragons of wit and fantasy; such qualities were life-giving in wartime. In 1942 at Ranby the emphasis was on gaiety in the old sense.

Many of the denizens of The Juke Box went on to be killed or wounded in Italy – Timmy Lloyd, one of the occupants of The Juke Box room, was shot at point-blank range when leading a patrol; Charlie Morpeth had a leg blown off in a minefield. Bunny Roger, who had been famous as a fashionable milliner before the war and was old enough not to be required to do any fighting, became renowned once more in Italy for the story that he, having become impatient with his regulation officer's pistol, had seized a rifle from one of his men and, after a brief reminder from his corporal as to how it worked, had shot a German at an almost impossible range. Raleigh Trevelyan, my companion in the cavortings in the Peak District, was grievously wounded in the hand-to-hand fighting at Anzio. Once when he and I were out with our platoons playing our catching-and-rescuing games I came across him in the early morning looking pleased and I said to him 'Raleigh, you're looking very starry-eyed!' and he said 'I've been seduced by my sergeant.' This may or may not have been a metaphor.

I wrote to my friend Timmy –

My darling platoon is now very much to my liking. They spend most of their time on training either killing chickens or stealing eggs, of which they give me a goodly portion, so I pretend very hard not to notice, though they would steal just the same if I did. And we have riotous games of football during recreational training, when it is their sole objective to trip me up and sit on me whether I have the ball or not. Which I enjoy because some of them are rather attrac.

And later —

My flesh is being torn from my bones by the icy gales which come whipping over these bloody hills.

We were sent off to a colliery in our trucks to pick up cinders to mend a road. The colliery had cinders in plenty, but also a considerable amount of unwanted coal. The first truckload of cinders was a failure, so we were told – no more cinders. Yes but plenty more coal, we bellowed! and rushed off to load up. The platoon took the coal hopefully round to their barrack room. That's a good joke! I said: and had them take it round to my room in the mess. Which they did in bulk, and filled the place with the filthy stuff. Later, of course, I found that it wasn't coal at all but slate, and would by no means burn. Thus my room is filled to overflowing with rank black rock and no hope of getting rid of it. It has also irretrievably blocked the

> stove in its refusal to burn. So the laugh was on me;
> but my platoon love me all the same.

This was the gay style. I reported to my sister that to my platoon I was known as 'Mad Mr Mosley.'

I had told my Aunt that I was becoming 'reasonably good' at delivering lectures in spite of my stammer, but I do not remember this being so. What I have vivid memories of is my gallant platoon being hard pressed not to roll about in the aisles while I gagged and contorted and my sergeant being driven eventually to bang on a table with his stick and shout – 'Don't laugh at the officer!'

In fact perhaps even my stammer was a help to me in what is called bonding with my men, who must have dreaded the style of a gung-ho disciplinarian. The way in which a junior officer was supposed to deal with an offender was by what was called 'putting him on a charge.' This meant that he was taken up in front of a senior officer for punishment. I found I had great reluctance to put anyone on a charge: reproof could be left to the verbal pyrotechnics of the sergeants; from whom, as I had learned when in the ranks, this sort of thing was easy to accept. It seemed to suit the men if they could see their officer in some sort of predicament equivalent to their own; then they might feel some responsibility for him as well as vice versa. This was a lesson I learnt that was most valuable later in the war.

The other ranks whom the junior officers came in most personal contact with were the batmen who did the chores in the officers' quarters; and they indeed seemed naturally to treat those who were nominally in charge of them like nannies with children. At the end of my time at Ranby, when I was away on

some course before going on embarkation leave, my faithful
batman Rifleman Baxter wrote to me –

> Dear Sir, thank you for your interesting letter on life
> at Cawthorne, it sounds an awful place, but I am not
> at all surprised because it is Yorks, and you can expect
> something of that sort from the cold wind prevailing,
> which leaves its unsunny mark on the countenance of
> the inhabitants. At a place like that you really need a
> good old soldier to make you comfortable, as they can
> always find ways and means. I hope that you are more
> fortunate than many others in having a decent chap
> who would also have to be a B-scrounger considering
> the wartime scarcity of certain necessities.

One of the slightly more senior officers I remember with
admiration and affection from Ranby was the Signals Officer,
Laurence Whistler, who would soon become famous for his
beautiful engravings on glass. One of Laurence's tasks was to
teach us the Morse Code. He would tap out the passages from
his favourite poems, and we had to unscramble these and write
them down: it was a help if one had some prior knowledge of
the piece concerned. Laurence was also a memorable wit. Once
when we were having dinner in the mess and a more than usually
unpalatable dish was placed in front of us, someone said 'What
on earth is this?' and Laurence said 'I think it's the Piece of Cod
that passeth all understanding.'

In counterpoint to both the gaiety and the drudgery of life at
Ranby, I carried on an earnest correspondence on the subject

of religion with both my aunt and father. My aunt was a fervent Christian: my father was not. My argument with my aunt had come about because she had become anxious that I was spending too many weekends perhaps pursuing 'gaiety' in London or at the homes of my friends rather than sticking to duty and commitment. I wrote –

> Somebody must have been whispering some very wicked things into your ear. The idea that a Rifle Brigade officer is not allowed to venture more than 5 miles from camp is so much precious nonsense. And to take Saturday night off – well, agreed it is against the rules, but similarly it is forbidden to wear anything except army underwear, and you will not find many level-headed men, let alone an officer, keeping within the bounds of that law. Seriously, even if anyone of any importance should know – and I cannot see that they should – they would care really very little. They might make it an excuse upon which to start a row if they were dissatisfied with my work, but otherwise, Lord, they don't mind.
>
> And the old red herring about shouldn't I suffer as my men – well really, that is a question that I settled to my own satisfaction a long time ago. Do my men mind? Heavens no. They ask me fondly after London every Monday morning. I show them that I can plunge around with them during the week, and do a great deal more work than they do too, and they judge me on my ability to handle them, and not on the amount

of self-suffering I can impose upon myself when off duty. Surely this 'moan moan and let's all be miserable together' idea is horribly wrong. And thank God I truly believe that the men realise it is too.

And I had such an enjoyable weekend! A very good party on Saturday night . . .

And then later, after my Aunt had sent me a copy of a speech she had made to an assemblage of bishops –

Of course I agree entirely that there is no hope for the world and the progress of our civilisation if we move and live guided merely by political or economic considerations. Thus you say that belief in religion and in a Church is essential. But you are anxious to centre this necessary Faith in the doctrine of Christianity as it is interpreted by the Church of England today, and in this I find it impossible to follow you.

Doctrine as interpreted by the C of E seems to me to be this – whether one takes the doctrine of Original Sin literally or metaphorically, it appears that God created man with a proclivity to sin, so man sinned, and continued to wallow in his sin for many gloomy centuries. Then at a given moment God sends his son down to earth in human form, and by his voluntary death the Son of God takes the sins of the world upon his shoulders, and the world is left free from sin. Thus has the ultimate purpose of the world been fulfilled by the life and death of Christ? If so, what is there

here upon which we can build a faith for the future? What can we do except sit gloomily and ruminate upon the past, and wait until in the pangs of the aftermath of fulfilment we finally destroy ourselves? The early Christians clearly believed that the purpose of the world had been fulfilled in Jesus, and they hourly expected the end of the world. We were made sinful: all we can do is to pray that Christ will come a second time more swiftly to consummate us.

You will notice that all the way through this argument I have tried to use the phrases 'the doctrine of the C of E,' or 'Christianity as interpreted by the Church.' I have never condemned Christianity itself, for I too believe that in the story of Christ's life and teaching there may lie the foundation of our necessary Faith.

What are the facts of Christ's life as far as we are able to ascertain them? He came into the world as a human man born of a human woman. By his personality and teaching he won a great and devoted following and performed many so-called miracles. Through his own intellectual exertions and his emotional experiences he raised his human personality to such a state of perfection that he realised that he himself might be called God. It was the agony in Gethsemane which showed him this, and it was then that he realised that in becoming perfect man he had become God, and that it was time for him to die and to become God in form as well as in reality. Those are the facts of Christ's life. The rest is either mythical or incidental.

Now here is the foundation for a faith for the future, a hope for man as an individual. This is the message of Jesus – he shows that in man is the seed of God, and that is through the exertions and understanding of the individual that the state of perfection can be reached. Make yourself perfect first, and then with the love that you would thereby acquire you would be able to make others perfect. He was always a supreme individualist, and the idea of absolute servility of mind to a mystical and dogmatic Church seems entirely against his nature.

These are the impressions that a somewhat irregular Church attendance and a little reading here and there have given me. My mind is not made up, and I hope it will never be, for one should never settle one's opinions, but always be seeking and searching for the Truth.

These ruminations were an attempt to escape from the wearisome routine of everyday reality? A determined effort to find a system of truth beyond the meaninglessness of anarchy? My father professed an interest in religion: he had the idea of a synthesis between Christianity and some sort of Nietzschean elitism. He had introduced me to Nietzsche when he had been reading his work in Holloway; but from the beginning of my own reading of Nietzsche I had the impression that my father was misunderstanding him as well as, more expectedly, Christianity.

I wrote to him from Ranby –

> I believe that Christ recognises his elect just as much
> as Nietzsche would like us to recognise his. N's con-
> tention that the *Ubermensch* were 'beyond good and
> evil' is of far greater significance than 'above moral-
> ity.' To be above morality is merely to be sufficiently
> civilised to be able to do without a conventional code
> of behaviour. To be 'beyond good and evil' is to see
> that such values (both ethical and religious) can be
> based on entirely different standards.
>
> With Nietzsche's values I have very little sympa-
> thy. 'Heiterkeit' (serenity) – yes, that is perhaps the
> most desirable quality that any mortal can posses. But
> 'Harte' – why always the emphasis in domination and
> power through hardness? There is no beauty, and I
> would say very little nobility, in 'Harte.'
>
> But I have wandered from the point. When I began
> to talk about 'beyond good and evil' I meant to go
> on to suggest that God is 'beyond G and E,' in the
> sense that it is obvious that his values are based upon
> entirely different standards to our own. And might
> not this be the answer to the problem of suffering to
> which we are so faintly now trying to find a solution?
> All our ethical systems and philosophies on earth are
> involved so entirely within the necessary limits of our
> own assessments of good and evil that I do not think
> that we, in such an elementary state of mental devel-
> opment, can have any close comprehension of God's

conceptions and values. The jump from 'within G and E' to 'beyond G and E' is so great that at the moment I believe it is beyond the powers of our understanding to see what lies upon the other side. When man has developed sufficiently to take this step he will be superman indeed, and close to God; but it seems that we are extremely (though not infinitely) far from it now.

I have become involved in a correspondence upon the Church with Aunty Nina. She was rather sensible about my fierce attack on the C of E, but one of her East End priests to whom she sent on my letter wrote me the most absurdly half-witted reply which only aggravated the grievance. I really do believe that these men do not understand what they say — which perhaps is best, for it is happier for them to be charged with ignorance and stupidity than with gross perversion and distortion. I'm afraid Nina thinks I have become over-influenced by Nietzsche. Which is untrue, for as I have said, with N's ethical values I have no sympathy.

Later however I learned that my anti-C of E diatribe had been sent by my other aunt, my mother's younger sister Baba, to her own favourite priest who happened to be a Father Talbot, Superior of the Anglican Community of the Resurrection — which, as things turned out, was to play a large and vital part in my life years later. I wrote to my father —

Baba's priest was a very good find — far less bogus than Nina's, and very tolerant of my rather wild and woolly criticism. I seem to spend most of my spare time writing long and intricate religious letters; which does not help very much. Like GBS I ask the most searching questions, attempt far too vaguely to answer them, and finish in much the same muddle as I began. But it does keep one's mind feebly ticking over, when one might, in the circumstances, so easily be mentally dead.

In August I wrote to my aunt to say that at the end of the month I would be coming on embarkation leave before being sent abroad to heaven knows where. My aunt and my sister Vivien and my brother Michael and our old Nanny, who was now housekeeper and cook, would be staying in a small holiday house on the north Cornwall coast, and I said I would join them there. I wrote – 'Eventually one will have to look at the world objectively and to decide what is to be one's relation to it; whether to fight the horror or run from it; to search for perfection in the solitude of one's own beliefs, or in the greater struggle for external fulfilment. At the moment however everything is unkindly settled for me, and thus all I can do is sulk or giggle.'

In Cornwall we swam and surfed and picnicked and climbed about on the rocks: we played cards in the evening: we had a good time. I was with people whom I had spent the best part of my life with and whom I loved. But it seemed that we did not quite know what to say to each other about my going off to war: what can one say? My aunt wrote in her diary that I was defensive about my father and was 'shatteringly crude and offensive about Christ.' Perhaps it was not possible for me after all just to sulk or giggle.

One of the last things I did before embarking on the troop-ship at Liverpool was to go with my grandmother to the Home Office and put in a request to a high-up official that my father should be released from prison: he could surely, we argued, no longer be considered a security risk. And he had phlebitis, which was getting worse, and his doctor had said that without a reasonable chance of exercise he might die. Watching the Home Office Official I felt I could see the levers of his mind clicking this way and that: but whether to the unlocking of prison doors or not, I could not tell. My grandmother said 'This is his son who is going off to war.' I wondered – Could it make any difference, my going off to war?

The war in North Africa had been over for some months. The British and Americans had landed at Casablanca, Oran, and Algiers in November 1942, and had headed east to link up with the advance of the British across the desert in the west after the victory at El Alamein in October. Hitler had declared war on America in December 1941 at the time of the Japanese attack on Pearl Harbour; for a year the Americans had concentrated on fighting the Japanese in the Pacific. They had then, however, wanted to get a foothold in the war across the Atlantic. By this time the enemy in North Africa consisted almost entirely of Germans: the Italians had faded away after defeats by the British in the two previous years, and the German Afrika Corps under the command of General Rommel had taken over.

In May 1943 the Allied armies advancing from east and west met in Tunisia, and the Germans surrendered en masse. In July Sicily was invaded, where the opposition was again mainly German. By the end of August Sicily had been cleared, and the question was being debated amongst Allied leaders about whether, and how, Italy should be invaded. This was when my group of Rifle Brigade and KRRC officer reinforcements were setting out from Liverpool.

We seemed to sail far out into the Atlantic; where on earth could we be going? No one of course had told us: this was the style of wartime information. There were the inevitable rumours – we were going round the Cape of Good Hope; we were to join up with another convoy coming from America. This guess appeared to be correct, because one day there were suddenly other ships around us. Then someone said we must be in the Bay of Biscay because it was so rough; and one by one figures disappeared from the breakfast table, leaving myself and one or two other sturdy gluttons to consume their left-overs – bacon and eggs, bowls of fresh fruit that had not been seen in Britain for two or three years. Our ship, the *Vollendam*, was Dutch, and had recently been to New York where it had stocked up with provisions. I wrote to my sister – 'I suffer more from being vomited against than vomiting.'

We were discouraged from working off our self-indulgence on deck after dark because it was feared we might over-confidently light cigarettes which, we were assured, could be spotted by a U-boat miles away. Down in the stiflingly hot lower decks the mass of other ranks swayed and sweated in hammocks, and were sick. On a slightly higher level, in four-berth cabins, members of the old Juke Box clientele lay in comatose but still decorous states of undress. Then after a few days the weather cleared, and we thought we recognised the Rock of Gibralter on our left.

I wondered – Would we be like Aeneas who, on his way to Rome from Troy, had stopped off at Carthage, near Tunis, and had

had a fine time making love to Dido? But then he had abandoned her to carry on with war, and she had committed suicide.

It turned out that the *Vollendam* was heading for Philippeville, indeed somewhere half-way between Algiers and the old Carthage. I had arranged a code with my sister whereby I might be able to tell her in letters, without too obviously breaking the censorship regulations, where we landed up. My sister's and my mythology was less Greek or Roman than 1930s films; so from Algiers I wrote to her 'We might be able to visit Jean Gabin or Charles Boyer.'

But how little had the style of mythology changed from the time of the ancient Greeks! They had loved stories of suffering and war: we now in films loved stories of sacrifice and grief. Why were there no myths of people getting on sensibly with peace?

Near Philippeville we stayed for two months in a camp, four officers to a tent, among sand-dunes. We bathed in a dangerous sea; we drank red wine and played poker and bridge. For a while we enjoyed the holiday atmosphere. I wrote to my sister – 'Yesterday we played football in a temperature equivalent to the melting-point of flesh: ten effete and flabby young officers beat eleven horny old Scotsmen who have sulked most ungraciously ever since.'

But then it seems we got homesick because I and some others volunteered for the parachute regiment. We understood that to succeed in this would get us back to England for a while; but when tested I was judged to be too tall and too myopic. We were sent on manoeuvres with armoured cars in the desert; during one scrimmage with the 'enemy' I reported to my father – 'I captured an enormous Captain in a hush-hush job whose face seemed vaguely familiar. Unfortunately I treated him with respect, for it turned out to be Randolph Churchill. If I had known earlier I would have thrown him into a dungeon.' When I was a child Randolph Churchill had been a good friend of my father's; now he was no longer.

I began to have renewed fantasies about how, if or when I did eventually get into the fighting, it might indeed be sensible to be taken prisoner. What was this human lust for war? I had paid my respects to it: but I did not need to remain part of it forever. And in prison camp I might be able to spend the rest of the war profitably studying and practising writing. This was to a large extent a joke — yet not totally. The war really did seem to be as good as won; and what was the point of being killed in what seemed to be everyone's insistence on unconditional surrender or destruction? And surely my father was right when he said that the only real winners would be the Russians and Americans. I wrote to my sister — 'The whole thing is so obviously absurd, so tremendously ridiculous.'

My sister became my chief correspondent when I was abroad: I had no regular girlfriend. My sister and I had always been close as children, like orphans in a storm. As I grew older I felt allegiance to my small circle of school friends, but my sister was never excluded from the style and substance of this. From Philippeville I wrote to her —

Last week I was whirled away darkly at dead of night to guard some Italian prisoners, which I found most agreeable, the Italians waiting on me hand and foot, and me eating all the rations. Unfortunately my only companions were the most granite of Scotchmen, whom I found even harder to understand than the Italians. I was followed around by a flock of interpreters. Equally suddenly and darkly I was torn away yesterday, my rule at the prison camp I suppose having been too much like an operatic burlesque for the authorities. As I returned I met Anthony, very complacent in an ambulance, suffering from infectious diarrhoea, no doubt caused by the incredible quantity of food consumed, and complete lack of strength in the muscles. He is away at the hospital now, no doubt very comfortable and keeping the complaint well supplied with material.

Anthony had been my great friend from infant school days, with whom I had volunteered for the Parachute Regiment, and with whom I had even briefly discussed the idea of being taken prisoner.

We were allowed to send home one airmail letter a week: so I wrote to my sister very small on the flimsy paper and asked her to pass on my letters to other members of the family. I added – 'I doubt if many others will get as far as this without a weary shake of the head, even if you are able to.'

For the rest – my letters were full of the pleasures of a Mediterranean summer holiday – games of rounders on the beach, swimming out to a ghostly half-sunken wreck half a mile out at sea, in the evenings more of the old acting and paper games, then getting lost in the dark on the way back to the tent from the mess.

I reported that I had difficulty in communicating with the Italian waiters in the mess because the only line in Italian that I seemed easily to remember was 'Your tiny hand is frozen.' Then —

> I have at last been made to do some work, which is most tiresome. I plod around for miles over the most mountainous country, trying feebly to keep up with more great strapping Scotchmen who I suppose were born and bred upon such hills. How one's thighs wobble! Anthony is still having the most blissful time in hospital. There is absolutely nothing wrong with him, but they put him into a diphtheria ward by mistake, and so he is now in quarantine. But he is allowed out briefly, so we meet for enormous teas at the café. The latest horror is a plague of toads who have completely occupied our tent and croak furiously throughout the night. We had a great hunt yesterday and found one in my spongebag. Our screams could be heard for miles.

On one trip inland I caught a glimpse of the city of Constantine, which still remains in my mind as one of the most beautiful cities I have ever seen. On a road to the desert one suddenly comes across it glowing on its vast rock surrounded by a deep gorge. It seemed to be a place that war could not touch.

By this time the Allies had landed in Italy – both in the 'heel' at Taranto, and above the 'toe' at Salerno, from which Naples was occupied on October 1st. Mussolini had resigned in July; and in September the Italian government that had taken over from him had capitulated to the Allies. Then in October, as part of a deal with the Allies which assured it of reasonable terms, the Italian government declared war on Germany. The Allies had wondered if in this event the Germans would retreat from Italy; but instead they reinforced the troops that had withdrawn almost intact from Sicily, and they put up unexpectedly strong resistance at Salerno. They seemed in fact ready to fight all the way up the mountainous terrain of Italy. However the Allied landings on the east coast at Taranto had gone smoothly. I wrote to my sister –

> Oh the news, the palpitations, the chaos! I am leaving here at 4 A.M. tomorrow morning, in about 7 hours time, and I am not packed and all my fantastic amount of luggage is strewn about the place. I know not where I go. In quest of Vivien? [The 'Vivien' was the name of my father's motor boat stored in a cave near Naples] To the place in whose beginning is the home of Scarlett O'Hara?
>
> I will send you a new address as soon as I am at rest. I really must be off, down to the busy sea, but to hear the mermaids singing each to each? Not B. likely. Down to the squelch of giant squids, to the weary bleat of whales. Give my love to all. It will not be long before, ivy-crowned, I roar through Rome on an elephant.

So in November I set out with one or two others (though leaving Anthony in his hospital) on a troop-ship to Taranto. As we got close to the war a raging toothache overtook me: this was a calamity that seemed worse than the prospect of war. I learned later that at times of stress it was usually my teeth that savagely objected. There was no dentist on the boat; at Taranto there was one with a drill worked by a foot-pedal, and an extraction instrument like a pair of pliers. However he said there seemed nothing organically wrong with my tooth; so if pain was symbolic, should one not bear it? Perhaps thus death would be made to seem acceptable?

Myself and the group I had been travelling with had been earmarked to go to a Rifle Brigade Battalion which had suffered many casualties. But now we learned that this battalion was being sent home, and there were no more Rifle Brigade battalions in Italy, so we were to be parcelled out to other regiments in need of officers. This evoked mock alarm amongst some of our number: what – officers of a 'rifle' or 'black-button' regiment landing up with a common-or-garden 'brass-button' regiment? One of the Rifle Brigade friends I was with had a brother at Army Group Headquarters; he got in touch with him and asked – 'Please spare us this indignity, and arrange for us to be sent to some eco-friendly "black-button" regiment.' The brother said he understood our predicament (army morale was indeed kept up by such niceties) and he said he thought he might be able to get us into the 2nd Battalion of the London Irish Rifles, to be sure a black-button regiment, and which had done much fighting in North Africa and Sicily and was in need of officers. We thanked the brother. We had at least done something to affect our fate.

We moved towards the front line through Transit Camps referred to by acronyms which I do not now remember: in one of these, somewhere between Taranto and Bari, we got holed up for a month while we waited for our summons to join the London Irish Rifles. One day in the 'Information Tent' (so I recorded in the diary I had been keeping) I came across a paragraph in 'Home News of November 17th' which announced that 'Sir O. Mosley is to be released from prison for reasons of health.' My diary reaction to this news was 'O frabjous day calloo callay!' And then – 'It is now imperative for me to get home as soon as possible.' Did I think in some way that with the release of my father the point of my war was over?

With nothing military to do in the Transit Camp, and having been encouraged now to dream about the future, I spent time in looking at and writing in my diary, which I had begun at Ranby and in which I had tried to elaborate my ideas about Christianity and the 'perfectability' of man that I had written about with such abandon in letters to my aunt and to my father. But I saw how critical and abusive I had been and was being in my diary about many of the people I came across; and in some shame I wrote to the old friend with whom I had been in love at school – 'But I also say such rude things about myself that I can hardly read back without dropping a tear or two about what a horrible person I must be.' This was in recognition of the glibness of my ideas about perfectability?

I had carried with me from England a large canister of books in order to try to continue the task which I might have pursued at a university and which I had begun at Ranby – which was to read everything that was considered of note in English literature. Like this I might at least not be naïve in my ideas. So now in idleness in camps between Taranto and the front line I read voraciously: I listed in my diary – *Pendennis, Persuasion, The Scarlet Letter, The*

Mill on the Floss: also, continued from North Africa – Nietzsche and Plato. In one camp I found some of my old KRRC colleagues to argue with: I recorded – 'But I fail to dissuade them from the idea that the blind chaos of government will not end up in the ditch just because it is English. I say we are already in the ditch, and will the blind get us out of it?'

Then there appeared a further item in the *Eighth Army News* telling of crowds in London marching round Parliament Square and chanting 'We want Mosley' and 'Put him back.' So what did they want him for – to lynch him? In my diary I launched a tirade – 'People are either hollow or heavy wet sludge. What hope can there be for the world if Englishmen are thus, and one can find no one better than an Englishman?'

My toothache had gone, but I had acquired a festering raw patch on the sole of my foot which I took to be psychosomatic. Perhaps I would get gangrene, and would not need to go to a prison camp after all.

A bunch of letters had caught up with me from my sister. In them she told me of the furore surrounding my father's release from prison. There was graffiti everywhere demanding – Put Mosley back in gaol. This must have been hard for my sister doing war-work in her small-arms factory. But she was full of plans for getting the family back together again. She said that our father had gone to stay at a secret address to escape from demonstrators and the press. In order that I could write to him she would tell me where he was in code, which she hoped I would be as clever at deciphering as she had been about 'the home of Scarlett O'Hara.' He had gone to stay with 'a woman,' – 'Woman' being the Mitford nickname for one of Diana's sisters. My sister also told of night-bombing of London that had started up again ('all hell is let loose when the barrage starts up'); and of a violent quarrel between our two aunts, Irene and Baba, who were now totally not on speaking terms and looked like being so forever. 'The GREAT ROW twixt aunts goes drearily on, despite my gigantic efforts to achieve understanding. It is all so petty and futile, but neither will retract or climb down.' She told how she had taken one of her factory workmates to have coffee with my Aunt Irene 'Nina' who was now staying at the Dorchester Hotel, her house in Regent's Park having been bombed. The meeting went well – 'Auntie was superb, and Joyce came away saying "any aunt of yours would have to be a sport after all."'

I went with my would-be London Irish friend into Bari which I said was like 'a dirty edition of Bournemouth.' But we found there a concert performance of *Tosca*, and I rhapsodised – 'You sang as I have never heard anyone sing before. It was not your voice, not the great mastery of technique: just the throbbing rise and fall of the waves, and the beat of your burning tears.' Shortly before this I had written in my diary – 'I would like to know how well I can write.' Also 'I would like to know how original and imaginative I am compared to the very brilliant.' Well, I was only twenty.

One of our last resting places before we reached the London Irish Rifles was at Termoli, where I sat with my back against a medieval tower and looked at the 'pale frail metallic misty hardness of the sea,' and read T. S. Eliot. I wrote – 'I find him so infinitely more satisfying than the old Zephyr-Lethe boys. He has a wonderful ability to make the reader's mind dance to his song, to become part of it, to think in its terms, to lose itself in his eternity of a serene and yet imminent unreality – unreality of

atmosphere, while describing the very real – an artistic achievement of the very highest.' Well, I was trying.

And then – 'In even the most intelligent people I meet, or
whose books I read, there is a complete lack of unity in behaviour and thought, in faith and reason.' Indeed, true enough.

So far we had travelled up through Italy by train, which I
described to my sister as 'unutterable confusion – enormous
pregnant Italian matrons clambering into cattle-trucks and being
ejected by outraged British sergeant-majors; tiny children picking the pockets of half-witted Americans chewing gum; showers
of rotten oranges hurled at any Italian soldier daring to appear in
uniform. And in the middle of it all me – with an Italian girl aged
12 with tremendous breasts and false teeth on one side, and on
the other an Indian who – oh God! – has begun to dribble.'

So I and my friend decided to hitch-hike the rest of the way to
the front. At the last Transit Camp at which we stopped before
reaching the London Irish Rifles, on the adjutant's desk as I
clocked in there was a copy of *The Eighth Army News* with the
headlines (even here!) about the continuing protests about the
release from prison of my father. When I gave my name to the
adjutant he said without looking up – 'Not any relation to that
bastard?' I said 'Yes, actually.' He said quickly 'My dear fellow,
I'm so frightfully sorry!' I thought – Well after all there's not
much wrong with Englishmen.

But what about the London Irish?

The 2nd Battalion of the London Irish Rifles was part of The Irish Brigade, along with the 1st Royal Irish Fusiliers and the 6th Royal Inniskilling Fusiliers. The Brigade had come into being in January 1942 on the orders of Winston Churchill, who wanted to create a force in which men from all over Ireland could serve. The idea had come up against opposition from the government of Northern Ireland, who pointed out that there had been an Irish Brigade who had fought for the French against the English in the 17th century; also that the name would cause trouble now with the Irish Republic, Eire, which was neutral in the present war. Churchill insisted, and the Brigade was formed.

The London Irish Rifles had been a territorial regiment before the war, and at the time of the Munich crisis of 1938 the 2nd Battalion had been added to the 1st. By 1943 the 2nd LIR consisted of Irish from the north and volunteers from the south; also others from anywhere that it had picked up on the way. As part of the Irish Brigade the 2nd LIR had landed at Algiers in November 1942 and had been involved in the heavy fighting in the mountains that winter until the German surrender at Tunis in May 1943. They were then part of the army that invaded and cleared Sicily in July. They sailed for Italy in September 1943, landing first at Taranto and then moving on by sea up the eastern coast to Termoli, which I was to find such a haven of peace a few weeks later. In October Termoli was being heavily defended as the eastern end of the German winter Gustav Line. The 2nd London Irish joined in the fighting, and Termoli was taken. From there they moved by land up the coast overcoming strong opposition at the Trigno and the Sangro rivers. But with the success of all this the Irish Brigade as part of the Eighth Army in the east was finding itself dangerously ahead of the Allied Fifth Army on their western flank. The 2nd LIR were moved to what was supposed to be a more stable position in the central mountains. But there Allied troops were very thin on the ground and no one knew much about what the Germans were up to; though it was evident they were not simply retreating. Also it had begun to snow, was very cold, and the London Irish were equipped with no winter clothing.

I finally reached the rear echelons of the battalion on Christmas Eve 1943 in a mountain village called Pietro Montecorvino. I, aged twenty, and with no war experience, was due to take charge of a platoon of men mostly considerably older than myself who had been fighting for a year through North Africa, Sicily, and a third of the way up Italy, and were exhausted. The Rifle Brigade friend I had been travelling with was posted to a company in another village. So for the first time I was away from anyone I had been friends with.

The first thing that happened to me as I reported for duty at the adjutant's office was that my kit-bag with all my own warm clothing in it was stolen; I had left it propped against an outside wall. I felt this was a calamity worse than my toothache; more desperate than my closeness to the front line. I was told that any-thing left lying about was pinched in a flash by the impoverished villagers: I could understand this, but could also understand for a moment the urge that must have come upon some Germans for instance in occupied countries to take hostages and say – 'Give us back our property or we will shoot you one by one.' It was no consolation to tell myself that at least now with no winter clothing I would be in the same situation as my men.

What might have been a consolation was the next day's Christ-mas dinner, which consisted, I wrote in my diary, of 'turkey, pork, tinned plum pudding and whisky, on which everyone got drunk except me.' I was still appallingly priggish in my diary: I seemed to disapprove of anyone who was not of the type of my precious coteries from Ranby or Eton. I took refuge in admiring the beauty of the landscape; and on Boxing Day I recorded that I read the whole of *Chrome Yellow*.

(In old age I find it difficult to acknowledge the awfulness of much of my diary at this time. However, insofar as it seems to have taken the war to knock some of this out of me – this is part of the story.)

After Christmas I went to join one of the forward companies of the battalion, E Company, who were based in a village called Carpinone just behind the very sparsely held front line. Here again I found solace in the landscape – 'Three thousand feet up, we ourselves are infinitely little beneath the snow-lined mountains which arise fairy-like out of the grey-green scrub twelve miles away: we understand each other, these wrinkled pyramids and

I.' Well, possibly. But also there I met my company commander, Mervyn Davies, who was to play such a large part in my war, and perhaps in easing some of the pretentious stuffing out of me.

Mervyn was a Welshman, some five years older than I, who came from Camarthen and had been to school in Swansea. He had been commissioned into the Welsh Regiment and then when he had landed in North Africa had found himself assigned to the London Irish Rifles through much the same chain of circumstances as I. He had fought with them in Sicily and at Termoli and at the battle of the Trigno River; he chose to stay with them, as I was to do later. When I met him in the cold stone-lined room that was the officers' quarters in Carpinone, he was tall and quiet and watchful: I thought – Rather like Gary Cooper. How does one recognise someone who is going to play an important part in one's life? By some such instinct as that by which I had claimed to recognise my 'wrinkled pyramids'? He was unlike any of the friends I had had in the army or from school. My first reference to Mervyn in my diary was –'He has actually read *The Mill on the Floss*!'

We established a friendship through talking about books. He hoped, as I did, that the war would not totally disrupt required reading – required, that is, to try to understand what on earth humans were up to. We applied ourselves dutifully to army life, but hoped to gain a vision of what should make life valuable beyond it. In later life Mervyn became a barrister and then a High Court judge. I used to say that he was the first good man I had known.

The two battalions of the 2nd London Irish and the 1st Royal Irish Fusiliers were given the test of holding a line in the mountains some twelve miles long with platoons dotted here and there on isolated slopes. The Germans would be able to overlook most of these from a higher ridge beyond. The Allied left flank had been halted just short of Monte Cassino. It was in the centre that the line had become seriously undermanned.

In the mountains blizzards often made visibility almost impossible. When this happened E Company remained based in the village, but even then we had to go out on patrol each day supposedly to see what the enemy was up to. We would blunder through thick snow for two or three hours and then sit huddled under the lee of a snow-drift seeing nothing, until it was time to totter back to our room in the village where, with luck, wood had been collected for a fire. In my diary I would record anything unusual that had happened in the snow – 'Big moment when given baptism of fire by a few desultory shells and mortar bombs, none closer than 300 yards but horrible whine as they drop overhead.' Then back in the comfort of the village, Mervyn and I would hazard opinions about books. I recorded – 'Mervyn began to quote T. S. Eliot's "Footsteps echo in the memory . . ." and with what delight did I carry on with ". . . towards the door we never opened into the rose-garden."'

We had little contact with the local villagers, some of whom remained grimly huddled in their cellars. However to my sister I wrote that once I had 'ferreted out a famous Italian tenor who lives in the village, and we had the most glittering evening with him bellowing all the great arias too beautifully, accompanied by his brother-in-law on a watery piano.'

Then the weather cleared, and the time came for the LIR to go into semi-permanent positions in the hills. It was still very cold; none of us yet had suitable clothing; some of the men were getting frostbite. I had seen comparatively little of my platoon when we were in the village; they lived and ate and slept in a different part of our building, and perhaps I was shy of them because I felt they must see me as an ignorant intruder. And when we were on patrol the snow and the wind were such that it was difficult to speak, let alone to get to know anyone. And yet had I not glimpsed at Ranby that the functioning of a good platoon depended on the nurturing of trust and affection?

Our position in the hills was on a mountain called Montenero – a wooded slope rising to higher ground on the left and falling away to a valley in front. Across the valley, on a higher ridge, was what we understood to be a stretch of the German Winter Line. But we had not yet seen any Germans; and all we knew of them was from the occasional mortar and artillery shells which came whining and whooshing as if from nowhere.

The snow was too thick and the ground was too hard to make proper trenches; the men of the three sections of my platoon – 7 Platoon – made shelters in the snow as deep as they could; and in these they had to stay during the day and while on sentry duty at night. Each section consisted of a corporal and nominally ten men but often fewer owing to frostbite and sickness. Two men in each section were responsible for carrying and working a Bren machine-gun, and the rest were equipped with Lee-Enfield rifles not much developed since the First World War. At platoon headquarters there was myself and the sergeant and a runner, two men with a 2-inch mortar, and an operator for the radio which often did not work. Headquarters was in a tent with snow piled up outside it like an igloo, and inside a brazier which emitted smoke which should not be allowed to escape or it might betray our position. Here men from the sections who were not on sentry duty came to join us and try to sleep at night; the choice seemed to be between freezing and asphyxiation. Two or three times a night I would visit the sentries with a rum ration; and either my sergeant or I would try to sleep wearing the earphones of the wireless, which was our connection to company headquarters further down the slope on the right. During the day the men in my platoon would slither down the slope two or three at a time to the company cookhouse to eat stew out of a tin with a spoon; I might manage to have a brief chat with Mervyn. Each morning the section commanders assembled in my tent to receive their daily orders. E Company was scheduled to stay in these positions for periods of three days at a time.

On the first morning of our second period when my sergeant and section commanders were all in the tent getting their orders, an artillery shell or mortar bomb landed next to us or almost on top of us, wounding two or three and leaving us all dazed. I thought that I was wounded because I was spattered with blood; but this turned out to be from one of my corporals or my sergeant. I shouted the order to 'Stand to' – which meant that the people in the trenches would be ready to open fire. I looked out from the torn tent and saw ghostly figures coming down through the trees; they were dressed in white smocks and were making noises like wolves. I shouted an order as I had been taught – 'Enemy on the left, a hundred yards coming through, in the trees, open fire!' No one fired. I did not know what to do about this: it was not a situation we had been taught how to deal with at OCTU. The section leaders who had not been wounded were crawling back from the tent towards their trenches; my sergeant and I had a small slit-trench outside the tent which was where we were to go in an emergency. My wounded sergeant had slithered to this and was lying at the bottom so that there was no room for me to get under cover except by kneeling on top of him. I shouted my order again: why had no one told us what to do if orders to fire were not obeyed? Such an event was not thought possible? My sergeant said – 'Don't tell them to shoot, sir, or we'll all be killed!' I thought this was probably true: but was not that what we were here for? However if we didn't fire, yes, we might all be taken prisoner. And wasn't this just what at times I had imagined I was here for? Then I decided – or it was somehow decided for me – No, that is not what I am here for! And my view of the world seemed abruptly to change at that moment.

As an officer used to obeying regulations I was armed only with a pistol; officers were supposed to give orders for rifles and Bren guns to be fired, not themselves to be equipped to shoot. The Germans coming down through the trees were now almost upon us: still there was no one firing. I thought I should clamber out of my useless trench and crawl to one of the forward section positions where I could myself get a Bren gun working. I had got some way when more grenades started landing; I threw myself – or was propelled – into a snow-drift. I lay there immobile for a few seconds until there was someone jerking at the lanyard of the pistol round my neck; it was a German with a sub-machine-gun. I made it possible for him remove the lanyard and pistol from around my neck; but how in God's name had I got into such a situation – and one which I had even thought desirable? The experience was unbearable. I had to get away.

My platoon were being rounded up and put in a line, ready, presumably, to be marched down into the valley as prisoners and across to the German lines on the further ridge. I thought I would hang back, perhaps helping one of the wounded – there were the two or three who had been in the tent – and then at the end of the line I might find a chance to dodge away. The rest of E Company should by that time have realised what was happening and Mervyn would be coming up with the reserve platoon to counter-attack. If there was firing, I could pretend to be hit by a stray bullet and then roll over down the slope. It seemed unimaginable that I had ever thought I might like to be taken prisoner! I felt deep shame. I had been mad. I should be mad no longer.

There was a wounded man who needed to be helped. I murmured to him that we should try to get away. We were at the end of the line being chivvied by a German with a rifle and bayonet bringing up the rear. There began to be bullets flying about both from the Germans on the further ridge and from some of our E Company behind. I clutched my chest and fell. The German who had been following us came and prodded me with his bayonet. I got up quickly. But I was feeling that the whole of my life hung on these moments; if I did not get away now I would never get away from being a dishonourable fraud – someone who had just wanted to get into the war for the sake of propriety and then to get out of it. And would it not also look as if I were under the influence of my father? There were now more mortar bombs landing and I determined to do another and more spectacular death scene, rolling over and over down the slope like a snowball or a Shakespearean actor. This I proceeded to do. I rolled on and on till it seemed I might be overdoing it; I came to rest with my head against a rock. There I thought I should stay, no matter who came after me or what happened.

I wrote later in my diary that I was not afraid; that there were some lines of T. S. Eliot going through my head – 'And I have seen the eternal Footman hold my coat, and snicker, and in short I was afraid.' But I did not think I was: perhaps I was saying these lines like a mantra to stop myself being afraid – to put myself into the hands as it were of the eternal Footman. What has stayed in my memory is my taking careful interest in the crystalline formation of the rock an inch or two from my eyes; the taste of the ice-hard snow as I nibbled at it. How beautiful were these sensations! To be savoured as long as possible. At some distance ahead of me there was a genuinely wounded man who had dropped out from the line of prisoners and was lying in the snow; it seemed that he had been watching me, and he was now calling out for me to help him. I wanted to tell him to shut up: couldn't he see I was dead? Then I could see the German who had prodded me with his bayonet coming down the slope towards me; surely this time he would not just prod me; he had been decent enough the first time; was it not justifiable to shoot escaping prisoners? He came very close with his gun pointing down at me and I remember looking up at him: he was a big healthy man with a round face. Then there was a thump and a bang, and he fell down. It appeared that it was not me who had been shot, but the German, who lay in the snow a yard or so in front of me. He grunted for a time; then appeared to die.

What had happened, I became aware, was that Mervyn, coming up with the reserve platoon from behind, had seen the tail end of the prisoners being marched off over the hill and bringing up the rear a lone German who then branched off down the slope; so Mervyn had shot him – an extraordinary shot, I realised later, some two hundred yards with a standard Lee-Enfield rifle. Behind my rock I waited till everything seemed quiet; then I stood up and waved; and after a time Mervyn, whom I had recognised, waved back. I set off towards him plunging through the snow.

I could not afterwards be sure that the German would have shot me; but he would have had either to do that or to leave me; it was too late for him to prod me into the line of prisoners again; his colleagues were disappearing into the valley. And why had he taken such trouble to come after me, except to make sure that I was dead? I had certainly put myself in a position where he would have been justified in shooting me. So it seemed that Mervyn had saved my life.

Some fifty years later, when Mervyn and I were having lunch together and talking of old times, I asked him – 'But how did it look to you? Did you see me behind that rock? Did you recognise me when I stood up?' And Mervyn said 'No. I've never told this to you or to anyone before, but in fact when you stood up I thought you were another German, and I had you in my sights. But then, I just didn't want to do any more killing.'

So perhaps Mervyn had saved my life twice: once by doing his most remarkable shot, and then by not wanting to do any more killing.

I suppose it is inevitable that I should have to come to think that by this incident my life was changed. Some half-hidden part of myself had emerged and rejected a part of the person I had

been becoming – the part that had felt that war, duty, could be
seen in terms of personal convenience. I had discovered shame;
most unusual! And the demands of honour? Indeed one does
not talk about such things! But in my first experience of fighting almost the whole platoon for which I was responsible had
been taken prisoner, and in a manner which I had once imagined
desirable for myself. It was true that in the event I had gone to
some pains and risk to escape; but then I had been saved by the
grace of – what – the skill, care, coincidence, of another? And
so what should I learn from this – that if one risks what one feels
is necessary then luck may be on one's side? But would not one
day some act of restitution be demanded of me?

- 5 -

After this there is a lull, both in my memory and in my diary; also apparently in what on a larger scale was going on. I do not think we stayed in the central mountains much longer; we were told we would be moving to a base area to train for the big push north in the early spring. There were rumours even that we were to be sent home for a rest: soldiers keep up their spirits by such stories. Then in the event we settled in a pleasant complex of farm buildings near Capua, north of Naples, where we were to practise river-crossings and close-combat fighting amongst buildings.

I was aware that I was likely to be in trouble for the majority of my platoon at Montenero having been captured without firing a shot; even though I had managed to escape. Out of a platoon of twenty-one men only six had managed to avoid capture during the original assault; the wounded man who had fallen in front of me had survived. A request for an explanation for this debacle came from Divisional Headquarters, and I wrote a report: the men had been half frozen; a mortar-bomb had knocked out most of my platoon headquarters. It seemed that this was accepted, because I heard nothing more.

But I was haunted by the fact that my platoon had not obeyed my order to open fire; although if they had, as my wounded sergeant had pointed out, we would probably most of us have been killed. So what was to be learned from this – the inadequacy of officers' training which did not countenance the possibility of orders not being obeyed? The wisdom of men who saw the futility of an order which would result in their being killed to no good purpose? But morally? militarily? My feeling of shame had been heightened by my peculiar personal history to do with my father: what would emerge from my impression that I had been somewhat miraculously saved?

In the course of our training in the countryside near Capua I remembered what I had felt at Ranby – that for a junior officer to be on effective terms with his platoon what was required was more than a reliance upon orders; it was a two-way trust that had something of the nature of love. So I now set about fitting into the training programme of my platoon some of the stalking and catch-me-if-you-can games that I had played with Raleigh Trevelyan's platoon at Ranby – for did not war seem to be a horribly over-the-top version of a children's game? In these so-called exercises my platoon became known as being amazingly keen. In particular we became the champion team at river-crossings. I taught my crew in its flat-bottomed boat the canoeing chant from the film *Sanders of the River* – Oi ye o ko ho – or whatever; and we won most of our races. E Company, at the instigation of Mervyn, adopted a battle-cry – Woo-hoo Mahommet! – which was said to be the war-cry of the Parachute Regiment. We evolved a private language which replaced the ubiquitous use of the word 'fuck' with the word 'waggle'; this had to be allied to a suitable insouciant style – 'I say, just waggle over that hill, will you, and see if there are any wagglers on the other side?'

One of the highlights of this time was when the Brigade had captured from the Germans what was supposed to be an amphibious sort of jeep; this was to be given a short try-out on the river. The brigadier and the colonel and whatever other bigwig there was room for squeezed in; they proceeded in a stately manner down the bank into the water and then straight on to the bottom. To the dozens of watching and cheering men this was a great boost to morale.

My platoon was billeted in a large barn, and for the first time it was correct for me to live and eat and sleep with my men. The only concession to my supposedly superior status was that my thin mattress and blanket were set on top of a large chest like a coffin. When I was stretched out on this it could be assumed that I was asleep or no longer present; then the men could swear and grumble and carry on their ritual cross-talk. And I could listen and wonder about the nature of 'bonding'; what might be called communal love.

We were happy in our barn, but there had been difficulties in finding accommodation for the rest of the battalion. I wrote to my sister –

> I was sent ahead on an advance party to choose billets
> for the battalion – a most unpleasant job which entails
> throwing Italian families out of their homes and turn-
> ing a deaf ear to the calamitous ululations. One old

grandam who I bounced into the street had hysterics and I had a tricky five minutes controlling her convulsions. But accustomed as I am to family hysterics in all its forms, it was not long before she was resigned to her ignoble fate. It is strange how unfeeling one becomes – I suppose it is just that one ceases to think in terms of pity and mercy; if one didn't, tears would never cease to flow down harrowed cheeks. As it was the whole business was rather frantically funny – me hammering grim and Gestapo-like on the door, forcing my way through the welter of pigs and chickens which live in the best rooms on the ground floor of all these houses; up to the swarming family who live in 'orrible squalor in the attic; me ejaculating fiercely in French to an interpreter who passes on the information in even more flamboyant Italian. Then the racket really begins with the grandparents moaning in epileptic frenzy, the parents calling down all the heavens in wrath upon me, the children taking it as a good opportunity to scream and yell to their hearts' content and have a good kick at anyone they see; and finally the pig and donkeys and turkeys etc, who blare and cackle their ridiculous animal-grab noises up the stairs in disconcerting unison. But I, the stern jackbooted I, neither flinch nor relent.

But was this funny?

There were the usual rumours about what we were waiting for: it was now mid-March, and the big spring advance was held up. The Monastery at Monte Cassino, on its hill some thirty miles inland from the western coast, was proving to be an insuperable barrier. The Germans were said to be occupying it in force; though this was later found to be untrue. But they were dug in on the slopes and in the town beneath it, and all attempts in the autumn and winter to take it by direct assault had failed. The Americans of the Fifth Army had tried to bypass it by crossing the Rapido and Garigliano rivers to the south; but this had resulted in such heavy casualties that the Americans had had to withdraw. A more ambitious plan was then hatched to make a large-scale landing at Anzio, some fifty miles behind the German Gustav Line, thus cutting off Cassino and opening up the road to Rome. The landing at Anzio had gone in on January 22nd; but the initial success and advantage of surprise had not been followed up owing to timid generalship and the Germans had been able to regroup. So it was now the forces at Anzio that were in danger of being pushed back into the sea, and there were calls for renewed attacks on Monte Cassino to prevent this. Assaults by the New Zealand Division and the 4th Indian Division were planned for February; but before one of the divisional commanders would commit his troops he insisted that the Monastery should be heavily bombed. This was agreed by higher command; so the huge and beautiful eleventh-century monastery was needlessly flattened by repeated waves of heavy bombers and the Germans, who in accordance with an agreement with the Vatican had not been within it, were now able to occupy the rubble and construct defensive positions better than any that would have been available to them before. So that when the New Zealanders and Indians did attack in February, both assaults were a complete and calamitous failure.

The London Irish, standing by in Capua ready to exploit any breakthrough, heard rumours of all this; and were ready to believe, yes, that those in command could be so stupid. And then in March there was renewed heavy bombing: statistics later stated that eleven hundred tons of bombs were dropped by four hundred and fifty heavy bombers on and around the Monastery and town of Cassino for three and a half hours – after which attacks went in with as little success as ever. The bombing this time had made it impossible for Allied tanks to get over the rubble on the approaches to the town and the Rapido River.

General Fuller was later to write that the winter battle for Monte Cassino in 1943-44 was 'tactically the most absurd and strategically the most senseless of the whole war.'

The London Irish had been moved to a forward position by the river: we wondered if we were about to become the next wave of sacrificial victims. But there we stayed, because the tanks that were supposed to accompany us were stuck. Some time during this period I went back for a few days to a Casualty Clearing Station for treatment for a bad attack of piles. This seemed symbolic. From the CCS I wrote to my old prep-school friend –

> I am in hospital, or rather I am clinging to a collapsible bed and 3 thick blankets while a tempest of wind and rain fritters about me. We are supposed to be sheltered by the tent, but that gave up trying after the first icy blast, and it is now a matter between the elements and the individual.There is one lonely figure here who has no boots. He was carried in on a stretcher weeks, months, perhaps years ago; but they

carried him in with no boots. He was better within a very few days, but he had no boots, so he could not get out of bed to go away, and no one would lend him any boots. So he stays in bed and every morning the doctor comes round and says 'What is the matter with you?' And the lonely figure says 'I have no boots.' And the doctors clicks his tongue and takes the l.f.'s temperature and feels his pulse, and wanders sadly away; and the Man With No Boots lays in bed and dreams of enormous galoshes and waders and wooden clogs, but they will never let him out because he has No Boots.

The impertinent fools who are in authority in this place have seen fit to place me on what they call a Light Diet – an amount of food so indescribably paltry as would not satisfy one of the worms that operate in my stomach. But la! Once more is the Philistine confounded, for on either side of me are men suffering most horribly from malaria, who vomit food up as fast as they put it down, and I have, by a simple process of logic, explained to them how much more satisfactory it would be if I put their food down where it will stay and feed my worms, while they will be eased of the necessity to vomit. And thus I eat 2 men's rations and my worms are surfeited (but my pile too for that matter). Unfortunately the men continue to vomit, but on an empty stomach, which is much worse, but I really can't be bothered to explain any more to them; although I am afraid that one day they may vomit

themselves right away, and then I will not be able to
eat their food, about which I shall be very sorry.

I recovered. I rejoined the battalion who were still waiting by
the banks of the Rapido River because the tanks were still stuck.
So we were sent into the mountains to the northwest of the
Monastery to relieve a Free French battalion who in the winter
had outflanked the Monastery from this side, and had got as far
as Monte Castellone – a rocky ridge even higher (2,500 ft.) than
the Monastery hill and halfway round its back. But there the
French had had to stop because the other attacks had failed. The
higher command wanted to hold on to Castellone because from
there one could look down on the Monastery; but the Germans
were on even higher ground beyond, so they could look down on
Castellone; and any movement on it or to it could only take place
at night. And even then the Germans were shelling the ridge and
the approaches to it in the valley with great accuracy. And after
we had crossed the valley there was a four hour climb with mules
to carry the heaviest equipment up a steep and rocky track. The
shells continued but went whooshing over our heads on to the
headquarters' area below; but on the slippery track – it seemed
always to be raining – mules were likely to slip and fall into a
chasm, and if injured they had to be left with just the equipment
being rescued. When we reached the summit of Castellone the
shelling intensified and the French were, understandably, in a
hurry to get out. This was the chance for a usual English grumble
about French volatility.

It was too rocky to dig trenches on top of Castellone, so just
on the near slope the French had constructed shelters with stones

known as sangers — about five foot by four by four foot high. Within each of these during daylight hours at least two men were entombed; any movement visible from outside brought on the shelling. Most of the shells hit the ridge just short of the top sending up showers of stones; or went screeching over into the valley below. But once, I was convinced, one ricocheted horizontally off the roof of the sanger where my sergeant and I were huddled; bits of our roof collapsed, but there was no explosion.

Rations could only be distributed at night: so during the day my sergeant and I would face each other eating stew out of a tin and at some point — there was nothing else for it — we would use an empty tin to shit in. There were the inevitable jokes — can you tell the difference?

My sergeant and I would stretch and flex our muscles and sometimes give our opinions about our present predicament and the meaning of life. From the small opening of our sanger we could see the destroyed Monastery above and around which even now dive-bombers circled like lazy wasps; then swooped down for the sting. My sergeant and I agreed that it was a terrible crime to have bombed the Monastery; but if we were in command of attacking forces and we thought that bombing was going to save the lives of our men including ourselves — then possibly, yes, we would order it. I had carried a vastly heavy book up the mountain in my pack — I remember it as being *The Brothers Karamazov*. I read its convolutions with my body contorted to catch the scarce light.

At night we had to go on night patrols, which did not seem to make sense because we could not go more than a few yards over the top of the ridge without danger of slithering into a chasm. The army had an obsession about night patrols, believing that they kept troops on their toes: which in our cramped daytime conditions was possibly true. So we would creep out a short distance over the ridge and there find a suitable stone to sit on (I once found my 'stone' was a frozen corpse) and from there watch the firework display of tracer bullets and flares going on in the area of the town and the Monastery. Then every four days we would go back down into the valley for a day's rest and sleep – though the long climb down and back up the rocky path seemed to make the short break hardly worthwhile. After a month on Castellone we were relieved by a Polish regiment (with whom we professed to communicate better than with the French) and we returned to the area where we had been waiting before behind the Rapido River, where still nothing much seemed to be happening. But we were told that we could take turns to go on a few days' leave; and I chose to go to Maiori, on the southern side of the Sorrento Peninsula.

I had stopped writing my diary by this time; almost my last entry was about when I had been taken prisoner at Montenero. After this I wrote – 'It seems that this chronicle of an Unsentimental Journey has had its day:' So I remember almost nothing about my days at Maiori, except that the place was beautiful and that it was somewhere that my father and sister and stepmother and I had visited eight years ago. So what did I think now might be a sentimental journey? Perhaps after Montenero I should try to make some reappraisal of my relationship with my father?

In my correspondence with my father about Christianity and Nietzsche when I had been at Ranby, I had written –

I see everything as a possibility, and have not the conviction to decide what is Truth and what is Right. I do not see how one can ever have this conviction, and even if one has it, why should one presume that one's convictions are right. My reason tells me what theories are the most possible, the most likely, the most desirable; but it needs more than Reason to put any theory across; it needs a great Faith. And my Reason tells me that it is dangerous to trust in Faith, for how does one know that one's Faith is Right? And so I am stuck; and am likely to remain so, I feel, until I am old and wise enough to have Faith in my Reason.

When I had reached Italy and I had learnt of my father's release from prison I had felt it vital that I should make my home with him after the war. But then when shortly after I had been taken prisoner by the Germans and escaped, I felt that this in a sense was my liberation from my father: but also, strangely, that I was now able to express my gratitude to him – for having given me my taste and love for ideas; also given me perhaps by appreciating my outpourings, the confidence to be free of him. A few days after my experience at Montenero I had written him a letter in which I referred obliquely to the incident, then ended with a declaration so extravagantly sentimental that perhaps it could only be a farewell for what I was getting away from.

I had been wandering like Shaw's Caesar 'seeking the lost regions from which my birth into this world

exiled me.' It is true that I have found many islands
– immortal islands with the greatest friends that a
man ever had – but I was always without home within
the ocean of this spirit-world until one day I went to
Holloway to visit a stranger: – and then I knew that I
had found the 'lost regions'; that my home was always
where it had been destined to be, and that I was not
alone among the waters of eternity. And now I do
not believe that I can ever be entirely unhappy again:
destiny has taken us thus far; it cannot be that such
great promise is not to be fulfilled.

Such gratitude can be instilled by parental approval? But what
on earth its fulfilment might be will have to wait till the end of
this story.

In these war years I could hardly remember my father as the
person that I had indeed only caught glimpses of when I was a
child – the ranting belligerent political figure in his black shirt
or uniform; marching and strutting and roaring on platforms
and on the tops of vans; what on earth was it that had got into
him (rather, than, it seemed, what had he got into)? But for the
most part he had kept us children away from his politics. And
then in his letters to me from Holloway he was so calm, patient,
considerate. (I have published a selection of his letters to me
in the second volume of my biography of him, *Beyond the Pale*).
There is one passage however that comes to my mind now when
I look at the paradoxes of my father's personal life and his politics. This was when we had been discussing the nature of what
might be understood as 'beyond good and evil' when one was

considering the horrors and yet the apparent necessity of war. He had written –

> We are therefore driven back towards a conception of suffering – of all the phenomena that are shortly called evil in the experience of man – as fulfilling some creative purpose in the design of existence: back in fact to the Faustian Riddle, usually stated with the utmost complexity but for once with curious crudity in the Prologue in Heaven [in Goethe's *Faust*] when the Lord says to Mephistopheles – 'The activity of man can all too lightly slumber; therefore I give him a companion who stimulates and works and must, as Devil, create.' *Faust* is meant to cover the whole panorama of human experience; but I believe this to be, on the whole, the main thesis of its innumerable profundities.

And indeed from my father's inveterate cheerfulness in the calamitous failures and destruction of his politics – in his evident serenity even in prison – it does seem to me that he sometimes saw himself (as indeed others saw him) as a sort of pantomime black devil; who felt he had some God-given Mephistophelian role in putting over attitudes and points of view that were not otherwise being considered – alternative proposals to an all-too-easy traditional reliance on war; other forms of discipline and endeavour. And it also perhaps explains why my father could almost always laugh – at least with me – at the ridiculousness of much of wordly goings-on, even his own; and who would wish his biography to be written after his death by someone who had known and loved him indeed not for his politics but for what had been the wit and liveliness of his seeing his Mephistophelian role.

He hated war. His proposals to prevent it had involved — it is true — trying to turn the country into a sort of harmonious boy-scout's camp run by an impossibly benign elite. He at times even seemed to understand that this was not possible; but he thought it had to be tried. He used to tell the story of a conversation he had once had with Lord Beaverbrook, to whom he had said — 'You are lucky in England to have got me as a fascist leader: you might have got someone far worse!'

- 6 -

When I got back to the battalion they still had not moved, and it was now the first week in May; time was running out for the big push if there was to be any chance of it reaching the northern plain before winter. However we were now told that it had been decided to attack direct across the Rapido River to the south and thus bypass the Monastery and the town; and that the enemy's powers of observation from these would be blocked out by smoke shells. One wondered why this had not been thought of before.

We still had to wait while planes flew overhead and there was a huge artillery bombardment from guns just behind us such as there must have been, I imagined, in the First World War. Waiting with us were tanks with devices to clear mines and to bridge ditches; but the Engineers had first to go ahead to build a bridge which would carry tanks across the river. But the Germans were now returning the artillery fire, in particularly on the Engineers who while they were working could have little protection. So bridges kept on being damaged before completion

– and the waiting and shelling went on. This was the beginning of my first experience of large-scale warfare with tanks and planes and heavy artillery; and it was mind-numbing, like a tidal wave or the heart of a thunderstorm. One could not know what was happening because one's senses were cut off: there was too much noise to hear; too much violence in the air to look. One just found what shelter one could – in ditches and by hedgerows – and then stayed within oneself until the cataclysm might pass. Accounts of war are usually told from the point of view of senior officers who have made the plans and issued the orders and then try to contact one another to find out what is happening. But they have little chance of knowing this until the storm subsides, the tidal wave has retreated; and then they can observe what pieces of flotsam have been washed up here, what units of men or equipment have been carried by the hurricane and landed there. And then reports can be written about what plan has succeeded in the face of what determined opposition. There will be not much about what has failed. But some order will be made out of what has been a vast display of anarchy. It is the anarchy however that remains in the mind of an individual involved. His concern will have been to endure.

I do not know how long we waited behind the river – a single day or two – one tried to close one's mind as one closed one's eyes and ears. There came a new noise into the tumult – a ghastly wailing in the air like the cries of a celestial creature being flogged. This noise came from a German weapon that we had not come across before – a Nebelwerfer, a large-calibre multi-barrelled mortar, the noise of which when fired was said to have been specially designed to strike alarm and dismay into the hearts of the enemy. And then one could anxiously try to trace the trajectory to see where a bomb would land.

In the evening of whatever day it was the information got through that there was at last one bridge ready; so we set off to move into position to form the second wave of the attack. But so much of the ground was churned up and blocked by stuck tanks that we were forced off the track into the sodden fields; and my memory is that eventually we waded the river hanging on to ropes.

(Sixty years later however there was a television programme about the crossing of the Rapido River, and one of the pictures was of the one bridge (so the commentator said) which the German artillery had not destroyed; and I was sure I recognised this bridge – a slightly skew-whiff but sturdy Bailey Bridge on props, with planks or tree-trunks laid crosswise, and handrails to prevent at least humans sliding off. So had we made it to this bridge after all? Or just watched tanks sliding off. Memory slips and wobbles.)

We crossed the river one way or another, but by now it was almost dark. So we had to dig in or find a place where others had dug in previously; then try to sleep before the Irish Brigade formed the spearhead of the major breakthrough in the morning. My platoon found an abandoned German defensive position where there might or might not be booby traps; in one of the dug-outs was a badly wounded German who had been left and was evidently dying. While my platoon settled in I tried to attend to him and understand what he was saying. He clung to me and spoke imploringly about 'Das Brief.' I found a letter that appeared to be to his wife or his sweetheart and I promised to get it posted, which I said should be possible through the Red Cross. Then he died.

In the battles for Cassino, and of the Rapido River and the Liri Valley that followed, there were numerous demonstrations of the fact that in Italy at least there was no hatred between front-line troops on either side – in fact almost the opposite. John Horsfall, who became battalion commander of the 2nd London Irish later that day when our colonel was killed, tells in his book *Fling Our Banner to the Wind* of the camaraderie between German prisoners taken by the Irish Brigade and those escorting them back across the river which was still under fire; of German medical officers and orderlies glad to help with the wounded of both sides at the Casualty Clearing Stations; even of a motor-mechanic prisoner being enrolled by the transport officer of the LIR to help repair his battered vehicles. Insofar as there was any animosity felt by front-line troops it was likely to be directed against politicians and senior officers at the base – who made such daft and ruinous plans and seldom seemed to learn from experience. But even towards them the feeling was more that we were all caught up in this wild maelstrom of human violence and history; there was no way of altering its overall style. All the individual could do was to get on with it and wonder – might nothing be done in future to prevent this savagery? In his book John Horsfall writes of the admiration he felt for the Germans who had held on and resisted at Cassino in spite of the bombings: such a sentiment was commonplace, as was the admiration of the Germans (so it was said later) for the Allied troops who kept on attacking and being mown down almost in the manner of the First War Battle of the Somme. But

these views and emotions did not seem to be experienced by
politicians and officers at the base.

The day after our crossing of the Rapido we were on stand-by
all day to take the lead in the big push to the north. The starting time for this kept being, as usual, postponed. There were
said to be not enough tanks yet across the river; the blocking-off
of the Monastery by smoke had to be renewed. When we had
been crossing the river the smoke had often enveloped us like a
fog: now in the clearer morning air the Monastery floated like
a celestial city above a fitful low-lying cloud. During the day we
moved closer to our leading positions; but even with the smoke
clearing it was difficult to make out anything of the larger picture. The Liri River was a tributary of the Rapido running into it
from the north: the landscape of the valley was a pleasant one of
low undulations and clumps of trees. All we knew of the battle
was from what we heard, and endured; from what seemed to be
the random violence of exploding shells and the wailing of the
Nebelwerfers which we had christened Moaning Minnies. We
learned that our commanding officer, Colonel Goff, had been
killed by a shell from one of these while trying to see what lay
ahead; also killed with him was the commanding officer of the
tank regiment appointed to work with us. We had to dig new
trenches to give us temporary shelter close to our starting point;
the start was put back from 3 o'clock in the afternoon to 7.30
in the evening and then to first light the next morning. So we
stayed in our shallow trenches for another night and listened to
the Moaning Minnies and watched the fireflies that seemed to
exist in a different dimension to that of the flares and explosions
and tracer bullets – flickering like those particles that are said to

exist for a millionth of a second and then disappear – while the violence was eternal. Then at first light there was the Monastery again like the celestial city now ready to receive us.

Throughout the night we had been given extra rum rations: now we were told there would be a hot meal to send us off. When this arrived I was standing up in my shallow trench doling out portions of stew from a canister to men of my platoon who came crawling up with their mess tins; there had been an increase of machine-gun fire at first light, but one had stopped trying to work out where it was coming from or where it was going. When I had doled out the rations there was a bit left over in the bottom of the canister so I thought, reasonably, that the least risky thing for everyone would be for me to take a second helping for myself. I had reached out my hand to do this when I was given what seemed to be a gigantic slap on the wrist – an admonition from a celestial nanny telling me not to stretch? I realised that I had been hit in the wrist by a stray bullet or piece of shrapnel. The wound did not hurt much, but it bled, and the end of my arm hung limp. It seemed that a bone must have been broken. People from my platoon headquarters came to have a look. A field-dressing was applied but did not stop the bleeding; it seemed that what was required was proper bandaging and a splint. There was a brief discussion about what I should do; there was still no word or sign of the attack getting under way. I thought that at least I should go to Company headquarters and let Mervyn know and show the medical NCO what had happened. However if I were a First-World-War hero, would I not tell no one and just stagger on? When Mervyn saw my wound he asked me to wait for a while because he needed me; but then when the attack was still not ordered he agreed that I should go to the medical officer at battalion headquarters and get the wound properly treated. So I left my sergeant, Sergeant Mayo, in charge of my platoon, and wandered off through the smoke and bits of flying metal. Then when I found the medical officer, Rhys Evans, he said there was no question of my carrying on; he gave me injections and dressed the wound and laid me on a stretcher until transport would be available to take me back across the river. The injections made me drowsy; perhaps it was then that I saw the Bailey Bridge that we crossed in my dreams. But I remember thinking – Should I be feeling grateful or guilty for that slap on the wrist as if it were from a celestial nanny? Or later – Of course, both.

People who survive in battle while others die sometimes say that they feel guilty; but unless there are particular circumstances this seems senseless: the whole experience is one of it being totally out of one's control. The myth of the bullet that has one's name on it often seems appropriate; so why not an image of an unaccountable angel nanny? So long as one remembers that metaphors, however true, are not literal.

So I passed quickly through Casualty Clearing Stations and was ferried all the way back to a hospital near Naples where I stayed for two weeks, and had an operation to set the fractures in my wrist. And it was there that I learned, in a letter from Mervyn, that some time after I had left him the attack had finally gone in, and the battalion had taken its objective, but had suffered many casualties, including Sergeant Mayo and several members of my platoon headquarters, who had suffered a direct hit from a mortar and been killed. And this was the reality, whatever metaphor one chooses.

Mervyn wrote —

Dear Nick, thank you very much for your letter. I had been looking forward to hearing from you which made it all the nicer. I am glad your arm is not too frightful. After you had gone I imagined that it was much worse than my first impression, and began to calculate how you would fare with one arm and, if it were your right arm (for I could not remember which it was), whether you would ever be able to shave with your left hand. Then I thought, well, he does some things with his left arm so maybe it will not be so bad. Really, though, do let me know that it will be quite workable again. Was it very painful? Do not say that your agony was acute and intense for I shall not believe you, but I am sure it must have been trying because it probably throbbed and kept you awake for days.

I do not know whether you thought me rather intense in not telling you to go back right away as I should have done. But really it was that I relied on you to such an extent that morning when we had so few fellows who I knew would 'go.' The show went extremely well. Jock and Desmond Fay both did very well. We lost Mayo, Henshaw, O'Reilly, Keegan and Cpl Williams. All these were killed during or soon after attack. As usual one didn't think a great deal about it at the time, but later the realisation beings to appall one. Michael Clarke was killed, Geoff Searles wounded rather badly in the arm, John Culverhouse and Terry O'Connor were also wounded but not too badly. Lovatt was slightly wounded. Sorry to give you all this rather depressing news but I thought you would like to know and may not have heard. And anyway that is what has happened.

You say you will be back soon. Do come as soon as possible, for really it is not so bad, and now I have no one with whom to carry on abstruse discussions on Morality and the Cosmos. So you see your presence is necessary. I will end up now in case I become too tedious. Really I feel I could write for ages because I can write to you in a manner that is impossible in writing to folks in England. Do write again. If I am your way I will surely find out your luxurious quarters. Well there you are. Yours, Mervyn.

I grieved especially for Mayo, who was a good and beautiful man. Close comrades inscribed on the cross of his hastily dug grave – 'The finest sergeant there ever was.'

When I was in hospital I began writing a poem about the Battle of the Liri Valley, which for some time I was quite pleased with. But reading it now I wonder if it gives a true an impression of the battle as perhaps the laconic letter from Mervyn does. What is it about poetry: it prettifies tragedy? Makes palatable that which should be objected to and changed? Perhaps some prettification is necessary for humans to bear their predicament. Such questions have become my hobby-horses in later years. But then I have never considered myself a poet. However this is one of the only two or three decent poems I ever wrote, so I reproduce it here because, all right, poetry is an effort to make something sacramental out of the obscenity of war. And one should try to see what does or does not work.

Lacrima Liri
The cornfields wave toward the sky
And from above the clouds reply
With smiles of gentle sleepiness.
Below, the summer sun's caress
Lies softly on the silent plains
And deep with the sunken lanes
The trailing thorns hand down to dream
And slowly in the silver stream
The leaves of weary willows drift
And sway to lazy winds that lift
The heavy heads of drooping trees
With tenderness of silken breeze.

But Stranger, Stranger, don't you see
Behind each crimson-tinted tree
Within those hollow, haunted walls
And torn upon each thorn that falls
So gently, gently, groping down;
Beside the silent fields that crown
The sleepy summer's brittle glare
With ripples in the sun-swept air . . .

Stranger, don't you see that there
The devil's terror-laden breath

Suffuses all with taint of death?
That here one summer long ago
The silent lanes did slowly flow
With drops of dying hearts that bled
And drained the dying to the dead?
That here vain tears of frozen grief
Once trembled on each withered leaf
And hung from every tearing thorn;
And out amongst the golden corn
Blind eyes did strain in vain to see
The light that mocked their agony.

Well, does that work?

Does battle work?

- 7 -

I was in the hospital near Naples for two weeks. Then I got ten days' convalescent leave. The world that I was finding myself in seemed to veer between the extremes of hell and heaven: to be demonstrating, if one was to understand it, the need to compre-hend both possibilities.

I wrote to my father –

> My wanderings have taken me into what I think is the
> most beautiful place I have ever seen. You remember
> Ischia? – the lovely island opposite Capri which we
> visited in the 'Vivien' [my father's motor boat] and
> where the peasants welcomed us on the beach with
> smiles and bottles of sweet white wine. How I got
> here I hardly know. Sufficient to say that my way
> from the hospital back to the battalion seemed about
> to become so tedious that faced with a delay of ten
> days at a dreary reinforcement centre, I stormed up to
> the C.O. and demanded leave. He complied with sur-
> prising readiness, only stipulating that I would have

to find my own accommodation. From then on fate took charge. I arrived here yesterday evening from the preposterous barrel of a steamer . . . I was met by a smiling old man who took me to a clean white room with a balcony that looked out over the sea . . . the dinner that I ate that night was such as I have not dreamed of for years except in the noble precincts of Holloway. Today I strode over the high hills that run along the centre of this island: at Forio a crowd of children and old men gathered round me at the café begging for cigarettes and hoping to humour me by saying how wonderful the English were and how they hated Mussolini. I told them I was a fanatical admirer of Mussolini, and a hundred percent fascist, at which they stopped plaguing me for money. One little boy broke into the lusty strains of Giovanezza until he was hustled away by a policeman.

What I did not tell my father was that another small boy, about ten years old, had followed me round much of the island offering, with graphic gestures, to masturbate me – and looking surprised and hurt when I declined. In the Naples area in 1944 this was probably a profitable business; Allied soldiers were lectured regularly on the near certainly of getting venereal disease if they went with Naples prostitutes. I had given a lecture myself on the subject to my platoon, embellished with lurid illustrations of resulting physical deformities.

Back in Naples I met up with some old Rifle Brigade friends in the Officers' Club on the beautiful hill overlooking the bay. Together we enjoyed – I rhapsodised in a letter to my sister – 'exotic bathing parties in the gardens of the Winter Palace of the kings of Naples at Caserta; parties in limpid rock-bound pools surrounded by classical statues and pink champagne. We went sailing from the harbour at Posillipo; each night there was the Opera.'

It would have been impossible for me to exaggerate the joys of Opera in the magnificent Naples Opera House which had re-opened almost as soon as the Allies had taken over in 1943 and, so far as I know, continued in operation it for the rest of the war. Anyone in uniform could get in cheaply – into the royal box if there were no other seats – and once I remember even lingering for a time in the orchestra pit. Singers were in the full-blooded Neapolitan tradition, ready to give an immediate encore of an aria if the audience demanded it. This style was a revelation; I still sometimes miss it at Covent Garden. Then from Naples I went to see the Greek Temples at Paestum. I wrote to my father –

> I made the pilgrimage, some sixty miles hitchhiking over comparatively unfrequented roads, which meant that I arrived on the scene having walked the last three miles in the heat of the day. I came across the first temple quite unexpectedly rising rather bleakly from the bushes and long grass by the side of the road. In the suddenness of the discovery I think I was a little disappointed; it was such a cold and desolate ruin; the pillars looking rather thin and forlorn under the golden heat of an Italian midday sun. But then as I wandered up beneath the grey portico I caught a glimpse of the second temple – the only temple that

really matters at Paestum – a glimpse of gold more golden than the corn which shone about it; more serene and beautiful than any concentration of Italian sun. I rushed towards it in an ecstasy of wonder.

It would be impossible also to exaggerate the importance to me of being able to visit, whenever I had a break from war, the artistic treasures and beauties of Italy. They seemed to represent the efforts of humans for more than two thousand years to come to terms with their bewildering predicaments – for instance that of claiming that they wanted peace and yet landing up in war. The large temple at Paestum was built in the sixth century BC in honour of the goddess Hera – both wife and sister of Zeus – whose chief characteristic was a jealous and vindictive rage against anyone she disapproved of – particularly any other goddess or mortal of whom Zeus was fond. She presumably provided an explanation of the rage of this kind that bedevils humans. Temples were built to placate her – monuments to order and serenity – in the hope that by this there might be a means of safeguarding loved ones and oneself, since it had not been possible to eliminate rage and jealousy altogether. Later in Rome I took trouble to get into the out-of-bounds Sistine Chapel and there to see Michelangelo's depiction of the expulsion of humans from the Garden of Eden – or of their preferring to risk the freedom of being able to make their own choices rather than to submit to the confines of God's laws. So was making art the means by which humans could both honour their freedom and hope to assuage its consequences? Indeed not abrogate it! Even the operas I was so excited by – I mentioned Tosca again in a letter home

— seemed to be trying to bind up the wounds of human tragedy and absurdity by passionate incantation and melody.

Then on my twenty-first birthday in June I was in a train going up to rejoin my battalion which while I had been away had fought all the way from Cassino up past Rome and were now by Lake Trasimene in central Italy. I was travelling with a young volunteer officer from South Africa, Christopher Cramb, who was on his way to join the battalion. I was with him when we found we had a day free in Rome and so decided on some stratagem to get into the Sistine Chapel. We tagged on to the end of a line of Roman Catholic priests who were on their way to an audience with the Pope, and once inside the Vatican we flaked off and had been lying on our backs for some time looking at Michelangelo's ceiling before the Swiss Guards arrived to escort us out.

One of the attractions of war is surely that it offers chances to try out one's own brand of anarchy — protected from the social disapproval and penalties that would be incurred in peace.

In Rome I heard of Rifle Brigade friends who had been killed — Timmy Lloyd, one of the landlords of The Juke Box; Marcus Hawkins, who had been with me on my journey to the LIR. My old school friend Anthony, who had arrived in Italy just after me, had been wounded in the foot when his sergeant had trod on one of his own anti-personnel mines, and was now temporarily back in England. My South African friend and I heard that the 2nd LIR was coming back from Trasimene so we should wait for them in Rome: we managed some more sightseeing, then joined them at Tivoli with its beautiful fountains and gardens. There I heard of more London Irish friends who been killed or wounded. We were then told we were all going back to have six weeks' rest in Egypt.

So one learns to accept good fortune as well as bad. We travelled down to Taranto by train and then set sail across the Mediterranean to Alexandria, and went into a camp in the desert halfway between Cairo and the Suez Canal. This was a base from which we could take turns to go on leave to Cairo; but we were happy enough for a while just to hibernate in the desert. I wrote would-be amusing letters to my sister. These were my efforts I suppose to insist that I still thought war was something to make jokes about.

> When I was in Naples I tried to buy you some silk stockings. But what the hell was Italian for silk stockings? With extraordinary presence of mind I remembered Rossini's opera *La Gazza Ladra* which I have understood to mean The Silken Ladder. So without further ado I bellowed Gazza! Gazza! at a terrified youth behind a counter, and bared my elegant if slightly hairy leg. When he had recovered from the effect of this inspiring spectacle a brief but sharp discussion ensued during which he professed to understand that (a) I desired to see an orthopaedic surgeon; (b) that I wanted him to shave my legs; (c) that I was an exhibitionist; (d) that I was challenging him to show a more shapely leg himself. In the end, inevitably, he led me towards a brothel . . .

> On the boat I bought a pipe, to emphasise the 'outpost of empire' pose that I envisaged. But I puffed and blew with little success. The bowl grew white hot and the spittle bubbled merrily, and the smoke

burnt enough holes in my tongue to line the stomach
of a carpet.

Oh dear, these jokes, how they do go on!

Could you try to get me a book by Aldous Huxley
called *Point Counter Point*?

Mervyn went away to an education course in Beirut; so when
it came my turn to go to Cairo I went with another company
commander called Peter, who was an exuberant character with
a large wavy moustache and the reputation of an experienced
roué. We shared a room at Shepheard's Hotel. Cairo had for
long been under no threat from war, so it was once more an
exotic centre for people who were happy to be away from the
austerities of Britain, whether they were working at one of the
seemingly innumerable Middle Eastern headquarters, or were
passing through on postings or on leave. My companion Peter
was not much interested in seeing sights such as the Pyramids
and the Sphinx; his idea of being on leave was to go to nightclubs
and set about picking up women. For the nightclubs he found a
ready companion in me: about the further part of his agenda he
said – 'Don't worry, one of us can stay out of our hotel room
for an hour or two, and then vice versa.' I said I'd be happy to
do this for him, but I didn't think he'd need to do it for me. I
don't think he quite believed me. But we had much fun dining
under the stars in the garden at Shepheard's; getting drunk and
racing in carriages like chariots to the fashionable nightclubs on
the Gezira racecourse; 'playing Chopsticks' (I reported to my
sister) 'on the austere Grand Piano of the Club Royale Egyptian,
where it was explained that I was an indefatigable piano-tuner.'

Cairo was full of people enjoying the anarchy of war, and Peter soon found himself an accomplice of the sort that he required. She said she was (and from her looks even might have been) an Eastern European countess; and when I honoured my part of the bargain with by assuring them I would stay out of the hotel room for whatever time they needed, she said she was sure she could fix me up with someone later. I thanked her but said I would have a look round myself. I don't think it was just squeamishness about venereal disease, or even residual homosexuality, that made me so reticent about sex: I think I felt that it was love that was being cried out for in war; the naggings of sex one could surely deal with on one's own.

But as it happened I did meet someone while my friend Peter and his companion were up to whatever. There was a girl at the Gezira nightclub called Kitty Costello; we walked hand in hand round the racecourse under the stars, caressed by the hot desert wind, and we talked about love. And I must in some way have loved her, because I still remember her name. And we seemed to have got what we wanted. But about even this I had to make a joke to my sister: 'I said I was a ballet-dancer and executed an intricate pas-de-quatre in the middle of a racecourse.' My new friend Kitty and I did not plan to meet again.

I had a letter from Mervyn on his education course in Beirut –

> I thought I had better report on myself to you and also ask for your reassurance that you are not beating up the local clubs every day. This is a likeable place. The object of the course, so I am told, is to inspire an interest in citizenship. The chaps are earnest in

the extreme, and I am sure they could not play Up Jenkins even if they tried. They like reading well-thumbed works on economics.

We had to give lectures, so for the avoidance of work I have selected two obscure legal subjects on which there are library textbooks and I give an incredibly boring half-hour.

Beyrouth is pleasant enough: the swimming is good and I am sorry to say I have been hearty enough to bathe before breakfast. The hotels are pretty empty, most people having gone up into the hills. So that any adventures that might be likely to befall me are extremely unlikely.

Have you had leave? Do let me know how it goes and who you spent it with and who you had to avoid spending it with.

There is an excellent library. All the chaps make a dive for K. Marx, which leaves the whole of the poetry section for me. Also those nice books that were coming out in England on the paintings of folks like Van Dyke (Gogh?). So I sit reading John Donne and looking at Art photographs surrounded by scratching pens amassing copious notes on nutrition, public health, sewage and drainage. I wish you were here. We could put on a shocking prig act.

In Cairo there was trouble brewing between the troops on leave – the 78th Division of which the Irish Brigade were part – and the local population. This was August 1944 and it was felt that the war should be about to be over but it was not. The party-going became more obstreperous. We were told that we might bump into King Farouk in a night club, so we sat around and banged our glasses on the table and sang 'King Farouk King Farouk hang your bollocks on a hook.' Out in the street the troops were angry at being pickpocketed and ripped off by traders; and it was said that boot-blacks were flicking boot-polish on to their uniforms. In August there was a full-scale riot by troops of the 78th Division with vehicles being overturned and windows smashed. The new commanding officer of the LIR, Bala Bredin, was reported as saying 'There will be no peace until we have them safely back in the line.' So the rest period in Egypt for the whole Division was curtailed, and we found ourselves on our way back to Italy.

I wrote to my father – 'I'm not really sorry . . . I hope soon to be able to visit Florence and Pisa and Sienna, and perhaps in a little while there will be Venice or Nice.'

In Cairo I must have managed to do some sightseeing, because I wrote home that the Sphinx had 'a pile of anti-air-raid sandbags under his chin, which gave him the appearance of having toothache.'

The news from home was that my father and stepmother, having been released from prison, were now under house arrest in a rented house near Newbury, and could not travel for more than a few miles without police permission. But the family, consisting of my sister and younger brother and our two small half-brothers, were now having the chance to reassemble again. My sister wrote to me – 'We all went for a vast picnicking bicycling expedition: Daddy looks quite wonderful with a pair of clips on his trousers and an ancient cap turned back to front like a butcher's boy.' And then of a weekend to which she took my two old school friends who were temporarily back in England with wounds – 'We all sat around till 3.30 A.M. listening to Poppa discoursing fascinatingly on the theme of Will to (a) Comfort, (b) Power, (c) Achievement – Superman to the Child and so on – with a bit of Democracy v. Fascism thrown in.'

My own attitude to the war at this time was that it was just something to be got on with – no more questions about ethics or justification. And it seems that my father did not go on about the war much now either: he was thinking about what he would say or write when it was over. He had professed to be a fan of Nietzsche but he was also now a critic. His line was that what he had seen as the 'Will to Power' was a comparatively primitive affair; what was demanded of the 'higher type' of man was rather a 'Will to Achievement.' I had not been able to read much Nietzsche yet (his books were almost unobtainable in wartime England) but it seemed to me that my father had got his own reading wrong: what Nietzsche was on about was not the ability to exercise power over other people, but a power (if this was the word) over oneself. That is – one needed the ability with part of oneself to observe and be critical of other parts of oneself: and by this possibly to re-order them. But this my father did not seem to have recognised – although he did have a capacity, sometimes, to laugh at exaggerated parts of himself. I don't think I talked much with Mervyn about Nietzsche, but Mervyn seemed to me to illustrate, with his quiet and amused irony more of what Nietzsche meant by a 'higher' man than what had been envisaged by my father. I didn't talk much with Mervyn about my father; in later life he would say about him just – 'A man should have the courage to say what he thinks.'

In my own letters to my father during my time in Egypt I was still plunging about on difficult and not very well thought-out ground; but usually in efforts to understand the daft predicament of war in which I found myself.

> I think the Hellenists of the 18th and 19th centuries shrank from the acceptance of 'horror' in nature because they did not realise what far greater potentialities for horror there are in the unnatural man. To a sensitive spirit of this generation the ruthless sense of doom in nature is not a quarter so horrifying as the miserable sense of futility when in contact with the 'unnatural' man of the present day. Anyone who has fought in the last two wars must realise this. It is incredible that there are sane men who believe that by renouncing natural life they can alter it or be immune from it. But could they not learn to make deals with it?

And then –

> There is an interesting man in my Company called Desmond Fay who before the war was an active communist. He is intelligent and very reasonable; and when we feel earnest enough we talk of this and that. And the more we talk the less is the difference that I can see between the conceptions of the communist

and the fascist corporate state. But then the only training I have had in the theory of Fascism was in the Pamphlets that you sent me when I was to debate on the subject at the Abinger [my prep school] Debating Society.

In one of my letters that I wrote to my father at this time there is a short passage blacked out, intriguingly, by the censor. I had been describing my often hilarious week's leave in Cairo, and the last sentence before the black-out was – 'The best sport of all was being rude to the ignoble staff-officers of GHQ.'

To my sister, who had been wondering rather dolefully whether she should have a go at reading Nietzsche, I had written that my favourite line in *Also Sprach Zarathustra* was – 'I would believe only in a God who knew how to dance.'

NM on leave in Egypt soon after the purchase of his camera, August 1944

Above Officers and NCOs of E Company in Egypt, 1944

Below Fellow officers playing volleyball, Egypt, 1944

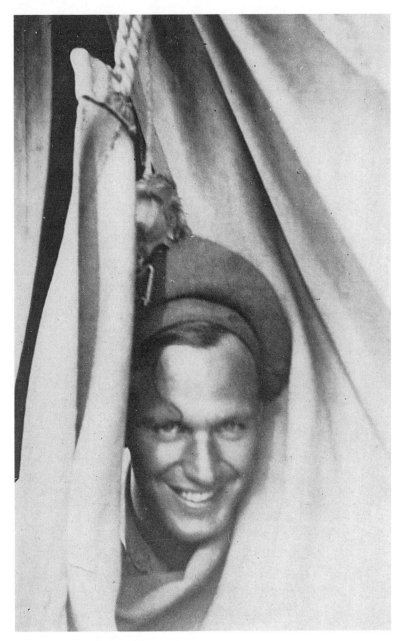

Mervyn Davies, Egypt, 1944

Above Back in Italy and waiting to go into battle, NM and Mervyn Davies with fellow officers, September 1944

Below E Company resting while on the march up to the line, Italy, October 1944

NM with Anthony in
the Naples flat after
NM's hospitalisation,
January 1945

Profile of Anthony in
front of the window of
NM's Naples flat,
January 1945

NM in Capri when the authorites had lost his papers, February 1945

Above Officers of 2nd Battalion London Irish Rifles on St Patrick's Day in Forli, northern Italy, March 1945

Below An officer celebrating on St Patrick's Day, March 1945

2nd Battalion London Irish Rifles on parade before the final push across the
northern Italian plain, April 1945

NM's platoon in 'Kangaroo' armoured troop carriers, northern Italy, April 1945

Above NM's platoon on a captured German vehicle, April 1945

Opposite page from top A British tank of the 9th Lancers near Ferrara in Italy, April 1945; A tank firing near Ferrara, April 1945; A German tank on fire near Ferrara, April 1945

NM in Ossiachersee, Austria, where he was stationed, July 1945

Above The billets on the lake at Ossiachersee, July 1945

Left to right NM looking out of the window of the officers' billet (wearing his medal ribbon), Austria 1945; NM in the lake at Ossiachersee, July 1945

NM on leave in Florence, 1944

A fellow officer accompanying NM on his way through Italy to fight the Japanese, July 1945

NM and Mervyn Davies at the end of the war in Italy, 1945

8

When we arrived back at Taranto in September I found that there was now a Rifle Brigade battalion in Italy, and a formal request that I should rejoin it. I was dismayed at the prospect of having to get to know, to become trusted by, a new platoon again – and indeed a new set of officers. And of course I did not want to lose my relationship with Mervyn. Also I had to come to appreciate the anarchic style of the London Irish, and did not want to go back to what I remembered as either the 'stuffiness' or indeed the affectations of the Rifle Brigade Mess at Ranby. So I told this to Mervyn, and we consulted with our C.O. Bala Bredin, and he put in a formal request, backed by the Brigadier, and a personal plea from me, that I should stay with the London Irish. And this was granted.

The situation in Italy was now that the Germans had been pushed back to the mountains north of Florence but still some distance short of Bologna and the northern plain. Here the Germans had planned and constructed their last-ditch defensive position – the Gothic Line. But it was not yet the end of September, and there was still time, it was thought, to break through before the winter rains made movement difficult. But the Allied armies had been seriously depleted by units being taken away for the somewhat pointless landings in the South of France in August; and the German armies in Northern Italy had been reinforced – although this was not known to the Allies at the time. The Allied command thought that with one more push the German resistance might collapse; Hitler's orders were in fact that there should be no vestige of collapse anywhere, whatever the cost. And then to cap all this the rains came early. By the start of October roads and tracks in the mountains were becoming a quagmire.

The Irish Brigade made their way up the eastern coast past Termoli to Fano, and from there turned inland to Castel del Rio on the road between Florence and Imola. The roads here were narrow mountain tracks with a cliff-face on one side and a precipice on the other: these were difficult enough for trucks and heavy lorries to negotiate at the best of times; if any traffic was coming from the opposite direction, or if a vehicle broke down, then movement became impossible. Once when the truck in which I was travelling spluttered to a halt and was holding up the huge column behind us, I got out to see what I might do to help the driver who had his head under the bonnet as if sheltering from the rain. I said 'What's wrong?' He said 'The fucking fucker's fucked.' This seemed a sufficient as well as poetic description.

After another hold-up in the dark, I remember clambering at the last minute unseen into the back of the truck which was carrying my platoon, amongst whom were some newly joined

reinforcements; and one of these asked of no one in particular
– 'What's the officer like then?' I was sure I was going to hear
something nice. Then after a while a voice in the dark just said
– 'Greedy.'

When we finally arrived at our destination, a village by a
rushing mountain stream, we heard, through a mixture of briefings and rumours, that there was a German strongpoint in the
Gothic Line that was holding up the Allied advance to the plain
rather as there had been at Cassino in the Gustav Line six months
ago; and it was to be the task of the 78th Division to take it. This
strongpoint was known as Monte Spaduro.

Spaduro was not quite the last mountain-ridge before the
northern plain, but it was in front of this that the Allied armies
were getting held up because it dominated the valleys leading up
to it. On the Allied side there had been a shuffling of divisions
between the Eighth Army based on the east coast and the Fifth
Army in the west, in an effort to make up for the depletion of
units for the landing in the South of France; but the arrival of
German reinforcements had so far made this breakthrough impossible. And now there was the rain.

When the 2nd LIR left their trucks after the long drive from
the Eastern coast we were off on a three hour slog up slippery
footpaths, and then into waterlogged slit-trenches at our destination. We were on a ridge facing and overlooked by Spaduro.
There was regular shelling. Around ruined farm buildings were
dead and decomposing farmyard animals; they swelled and burst,
releasing stench. And at night there was still the 'game' of going
out on patrol with instructions to find out about enemy positions;
in fact going as far as seemed reasonable and then sitting beside a

tree and watching shadows and listening to rustlings. And then, having spent enough time in what might be taken to be looking for enemy positions, coming back through our lines where there might be different people on sentry duty from those there has been when we had gone out, and so there was danger of their mistaking us for enemy and opening fire. And then we would report back to battalion headquarters – No sign of enemy activity – which was true enough; and we trusted that everyone would understand the rules of the game. This was a time when the most pressing threat seemed to be that of dysentery; but seldom serious enough for one to be carried away on a stretcher.

Other formations had been trying, and failing, to take Monte Spaduro. Then it was the turn of the Irish Brigade. It had for long been army lore that no one should move in the mountains except at night: daytime activity simply brought forth accurate machine-gun, mortar and artillery fire. But even at night in any settled position the enemy would have worked out their fixed-line fields of fire, and any attackers were likely to have become stuck in the mud of a valley and so would be sitting targets even in the dark. The rumours were that other formations who had attacked Spaduro at night had failed ruinously because of this. But it seemed that Allied Headquarters did not know what else to do.

Squatting in our tiny six-foot by three slit-trenches nothing much seemed to matter to us except the shelling and the rain. The Irish Fusiliers, it was said, had been sent into a full battalion night attack on Spaduro and had had to retreat with many casualties. The Inniskillings had been called away to do a diversion elsewhere. This left the London Irish for any further attempts.

But by this time the shelling on our inadequate trenches was so constant that we hardly cared. One shell landed so close to the top of my trench that the edges caved in and my back-pack was riddled with shrapnel, and the book I was currently reading – I cannot now remember what it was – had a piece of metal embedded deeply in it. At least I might be able to tell the story after the war about how it had stopped my being pierced to the heart.

One night we had gone down into a valley to give support to one of the large-scale attacks; we could see nothing, we got embedded in the deep mud, we seemed to be under accurate machine-gun fire from some forward enemy position on our right. We stayed where we were for a while; then struggled back.

The machine-gun fire had appeared to come mainly from a group of semi-ruined farmhouses and buildings on the spur of ground which stretched for some six hundred yards between the enemy and our positions. From these buildings accurate fire could be directed on fixed lines at the flanks of anyone in the valleys. We could see the farmstead in daylight if we were careful not to raise our heads too far. It began to dawn on everyone that Spaduro would never be taken unless the crossfire from this outpost was eliminated. On the map the farmhouse was called Casa Spinello. The London Irish were given the task of mounting a night attack on Casa Spinello – not head on, where there were likely to be minefields, but once again round the valley at the side.

I think everyone in Mervyn's company thought this would be useless; we would get stuck as we had got stuck before. Nevertheless off we went the next night in the driving rain; and this time we had not only to get down into the valley but supposedly

up the other side; and this in the cloying mud proved to be literally impossible. And our efforts of course alerted the Germans
in Spinello so that machine-gun and mortar-fire came down on
us where we were now in the open because we had been trying
not to shelter but to attack: and because we were frightened, and
almost didn't care anymore, we tended to huddle together; so
we suffered a regular toll of casualties. One of them was Christopher Cramb, the young South African volunteer who had been
with me in Rome. He was standing next to me and he called
out loudly – 'God have mercy on my soul' – and then fell and
died. Mervyn was trying to get through on the radio to demand
permission to withdraw; but he was told to continue with the
so-called attack. Then to his eternal credit Mervyn decided to
ignore this order, and on his own initiative he led us back up the
slope on our side of the valley, carrying our wounded and those
we could of our dead.

When Mervyn was summoned by the Colonel and the Brigadier to report on his withdrawal he said that they did not seem
to understand the futility of their tactics: we would never take
Spinello nor indeed Spaduro with cumbersome numbers of men
sliding down into a mud-trap at night and there remaining help-
less while they were shot at from Spinello. What was necessary,
he said, was for a small force of men to set off while it was still
light by as direct a route as possible to Spinello, keeping as far
as they could just under the shelter of the spur. Then when they
were as close to Spinello as they could get like this, they could
attack running fast across open ground. This should happen
shortly before the regular time of stand-to at dusk, when it was
almost inconceivable that the Germans would be expecting an

attack, so uncommon was any movement by day; and in fact it was possible that the Germans would be sleeping. Then, if this attack on Spinello was successful, there would be a chance of a major night attack on Spaduro succeeding.

The Colonel and the Brigadier listened to Mervyn and said – 'All right, you and your company try it.'

One of the other platoon commanders in our company was the young communist from Liverpool, Desmond Fay, with whom I had argued amicably about communism and fascism in Egypt. Desmond had been brave during the advance from Cassino, and had been awarded the Military Cross.

Now when Mervyn gathered us to tell us of his plans, he suggested that Desmond should go out in the early afternoon with just one or two men and try to find out what was the situation in Spinello – how many Germans were there, and what were their defensive positions: if possible he should bring back a prisoner who could be questioned. Then if Desmond's information was satisfactory, I with my platoon would lead an attack to capture the farmhouse and buildings – still in daylight, but just before the time when the Germans could be expected to be standing-to. Then if my attack was successful, the rest of the company would come up and we would hold Spinello during the night while the inevitable German counter-attacks came in, and while a large-scale Allied attack on Spaduro would go in with this time a chance of success because the cross-fire from Spinello would have been eliminated.

This scheme seemed to me both mad and yet, as it had done to Mervyn, to make some sense. But I wondered – Why has Mervyn chosen me to do the attack? Then – Oh yes, I see.

When I told my sergeant and my section commanders of this plan they too naturally thought it was mad: had we not been told never to move into the view of the enemy in daylight? I explained – Yes, but they will not believe that we could be so mad: they will not have properly woken from their daytime sleep; they will think they are dreaming. My section commanders and sergeant looked at me as if they thought they or I might be dreaming.

From a certain vantage point we could just see, by lifting our heads carefully, the farmhouse about a quarter of a mile away along the spur; some ruined farm buildings were on this side of it. We had a few hours to wait before Desmond set off on his patrol; after which it would almost certainly be our turn to go. We could pass the time by making sure that our weapons were in proper order; I had myself by this time acquired a Thompson sub-machine gun, which had the reputation at critical moments of being likely to jam. But not, surely, if one took enough trouble. There was time also to ruminate on the bizarreness of fate.

When I had been taken prisoner and had succeeded in my decision at any cost to try to escape, I had been helped by good fortune and by Mervyn. Then, later when I had been wounded South of Cassino, Sergeant Mayo, who had taken over from me had been killed. I had thought – All right, I am very lucky! but sooner or later there will be payback time. Something further will be demanded of me: either my luck will run out, or there will be some test why it should not.

So is not this the sort of thing that I have wanted, or needed, ever since most of my platoon were taken prisoner without firing a shot, even though I had managed to escape? I have needed a chance to show in a positive way a break from the cynical attitudes of my past; from the negative tendencies of my history. When Mervyn had come to tell me of his plans for my attack he had murmured 'This is an MC job.' This was army jargon for an assignment which, if it succeeded, might result in one's being recommended for a Military Cross; and if it failed one was likely to be dead.

So had Mervyn an instinct for what I might require?

(You think people don't ruminate on such things at such perilous moments? What else do they think about?)

Desmond Fay's patrol was amazingly successful. He went out with just his sergeant, and came back with a German prisoner who had been half asleep in a trench by the farm buildings. The German talked: he said that Spinello was held by about thirty men during the day; at night they were in contact with troops on the hills behind who came up with more machine-guns. There was some good news in this in that it seemed the Germans might not be in good heart if the man had been taken and talked so easily; but thirty men was a lot for my depleted platoon to take on; and would not the capture of this prisoner mean that his colleagues would now have been alerted? My platoon was down to fifteen men, what with sickness and injury; and when it was time for us to form up I wondered if there would be any who would say they could not go on. There was in fact only one, a senior corporal who lay in the bottom of his trench and said he could not move. I talked with him for a time, and then said – All right, don't. He would not have been much use in a platoon that was otherwise behaving so admirably. But I think we all felt we might be on a suicide mission.

I had two lance-corporals, Tomkinson and McClarnon, who with their sections would go with me into the attack. My sergeant would be with the Bren gun of the third section to give us covering fire. The rest of the Company would be ready to give more covering fire if necessary from the hill at the back.

Desmond was to start off with us to show us the way he had reconnoitred, keeping out of sight of the farmhouse by moving under the brow of the spur. But even here we would be in full view of the Germans on the hills beyond – so was it true they would be sleeping? Then for the last hundred yards or so we would have to break from the cover of the spur and run to the farm buildings across open ground; if the Germans had been alerted, this is what was likely to be suicidal.

We moved off in our meagre crocodile quite openly, like people hoping not to draw attention to themselves if they show sufficient insouciance. On our right we could look across the valleys that stretched away towards Imola and the promised land of the northern plain. For the first time in weeks the rain was holding off; it was almost a beautiful evening.

We got to the place beneath the spur which seemed nearest to the farmhouse and there we spread out and lined up. When I told the story later (I did not often do this) I used to say that I was frightened, yes, but what I was most frightened of was not being able to stand the fear: and then what would happen? The fabric of the mind would crack, and I would fall through? When I had felt close to death in the snow at Montenero all I had had to do was lie still: now I had to run forward. I saw that the Bren gun was in position to give us covering fire; then I gave the order to go.

I had been a fast runner at school, and now it was obviously in my interest to get into some sort of cover as soon as possible. The farm buildings were after all not much more than eighty yards away; this was not too bad a distance; but I was festooned with tommy-gun, spare magazines, grenades; and – and – never mind, just keep running! When I had almost reached the farm buildings I looked back and saw Corporal McClarnon's section a long way behind. I shouted 'Come on McClarnon!' He, a sturdy man with short legs, shouted 'I'm coming as fast as I can!' By this time Corporal Tomkinson had caught up with me; then a man with a gun popped up from the rubble of the farm buildings and Tomkinson fired at him and hit him and I sprayed with my tommy gun the buildings from where he had appeared. Then someone started shouting 'Don't shoot Johnny! Play the game Johnny!' So Tomkinson and I ran on. By this time grenades thrown from the farmhouse had started landing around us, so I called to McClarnon to take charge of any people in the buildings and Tomkinson and I got to the back wall of the farm-house. There was now a good deal of machine-gun and rifle fire, whether from Germans on the hills beyond or our own people giving us covering fire from the back, I could not tell. It was obviously urgent to get inside the cover of the house.

The farmhouse was one of those buildings on a slope which if you go into it on the ground floor at the back, this turns out to be the first floor at the front. There did not seem to be anyone in this first floor where we came to it; the main body of Ger-mans were evidently sheltering in the ground floor at the front. Grenades were being lobbed from round the sides of the house: I called to Tomkinson to go with his section round the right side while I went round on the left. A German had followed me from the farm building with his hands up smiling: I told him I had no time for him, and to go and find McClarnon. Then I came to a hole in the wall of the house: this led to a room which appeared to be empty. There was also a gap in the floor just beyond the hole through which I could see to the ground floor at the front. This room appeared to be empty too. Then three Germans appeared through a door at the front; they carried automatic weapons; they saw me through the holes in the floor and wall at the same time as I saw them; I fired first and shot two of them in the legs. The third ran out of the door at the front and one of the others hopped after him holding his leg; the other had fallen and lay where he fell. The magazine of my tommy-gun was now empty; I cursed myself for having spent so much ammunition firing blindly at the rubble of the buildings. I sheltered to one side of my hole while I fixed on a new magazine. By the time I had got back to where I could see down to the ground the second man I had hit in the legs had gone – presumably he had crawled out after the other two. So might I then be glad that I had had no more bullets in my magazine, and need not shoot him again? I called to McClarnon to leave two of his men to guard any prisoners from the buildings, then to come up with what was left of his section and go into and occupy the now empty upstairs and downstairs rooms on the left. This he did. Then I went to see how Tomkinson was doing on the right.

This side of the house was covered by German machine-guns from the hills beyond, and bullets were flying and chipping bits off the walls. Tomkinson had gone forward and taken shelter behind a well which was near the front of the house; his Bren-gunner had been hit and two of his men were dragging him back behind the house. I joined Tomkinson by the well but we could see no door into the house except the one on the left which Mc-Clarnon was now guarding. The right front of the house seemed to have collapsed; there was just an opening like a hole to a dug-out in the rubble. Bullets were chipping bits of stone around our heads so we threw a couple of grenades at the opening, and I retired in haste. Tomkinson stayed by the well; and when someone fired at him from the opening he stood up and fired what was left in his magazine back at it, before rejoining me in the shelter of the house. Then I sent him with the few men left of his section to join McClarnon who was occupying the rooms on the left.

The third section had by this time come up with my sergeant, and I went again with them to the right front corner because I thought we had to clear this – to take prisoner the Germans who seemed to have barricaded themselves into a basement through the opening in the ground-floor rubble, because surely our position would become untenable if they stayed underneath us during the night. My sergeant threw one grenade at the open-ing and then was hit by a stray bullet from the hills; he and his section retired to the back of the house. I was by the well firing blindly and absurdly at the German machine-gunners on the hill who were hundreds of yards out of my tommy-gun's range. I turned to the house again to throw one last grenade and there was a German who had crawled out of the opening like a hole and was facing me holding an automatic weapon and he fired at me at point-blank range and somehow missed. My magazine was now empty again so I did a flying leap back round the side of the house (I described this later as my 'Nijinsky leap') and I determined not to go round to the front again. We would have to hold on to what we had got until morning.

It seemed that we were in occupation of most of the farm-houses except the ground floor or basement on the right, which the Germans indeed seemed to have made impregnable. Above this on the right of the first floor there was a hayloft. From the upstairs room on the left I and others crawled into this loft to see how it could be occupied and defended; then the Germans below starting firing up through the floorboards. We jumped about like victims in the red-hot bull of Phalaris; we fired down through the floorboards; and then there were voices again – 'Don't shoot Johnny!' I tried to remember my schoolboy German – 'We will not shoot at you if you will not shoot at us!' Was there not a special conditional tense? And was I not using the word for 'shit' instead of 'shoot'? But what would be the difference! I seemed anyway to have got the message through, because for the rest of the evening and night there was no more shooting up or down through the floorboards.

By this time Mervyn had arrived with the rest of the company, and he insisted on going himself to have a look at the right front of the house where there was the opening to where the Germans remained; but he was almost immediately hit in the arm and leg and was pulled back under cover. I said I would get him back on a stretcher as soon as we had one; but he insisted he was all right, he could get back on his own – and it was vital that he should do this, because he could then explain the seri-ousness of our situation and could get reinforcements sent up. I would be intensely sorry to see him go, because I needed both

him personally and someone who would share the responsibility
for defending what we had taken now that night was coming in
and there were bound to be counter-attacks. But Desmond had
come up with Mervyn, and he was a senior lieutenant to me, so
he would nominally take over. Then Mervyn went hopping back
on one leg by the most direct route to our old positions; and it
turned out later that he had hopped unharmed straight through
a minefield. We became aware of this later when the reinforcements he sent up walked into the minefield and many were killed
or wounded and the rest never got through. This was a disaster
for them; but for us it seemed that there were already enough
of us crammed into the farmhouse, and Desmond agreed that
it would be crazy to consider digging trenches outside. So we
settled down to assess our situation.

We had what was left of the three platoons of our Company in
the two rooms one above the other on the left of the farmhouse
– some thirty men, ten of whom had wounds of some sort or
other – and nine Bren guns. We arranged these on the two floors
with a makeshift ladder between. Then we realised it was quite
dark.

During the night three or four counter-attacks did come in
from the further hills; but by this time we were experiencing
a strange exhilaration. We felt invulnerable, heroic; when we
heard Germans approaching we opened fire with all our weapons from every opening in all directions; I remember one man
who had lost his spectacles and could find no room at a window,
firing his rifle repeatedly straight up into the air. We yelled and
whooped our war-cry – Woo hoo Mahommet! – and blazed
away until the attacks seemed to fade away into the thin night

air. It was all quite like, yes, an apotheosis of a mad apocalyptic children's game. Only once I think did a German get right up to the wall of the house; he shot one of our men point-blank through a window. Grenades usually bounced off the walls and exploded outside. After a time things quietened down. Our wireless was not working, so at least we were out of touch with headquarters so they could not order us to do anything different.

There was the business of tending to the wounded. Amazingly, none of my platoon seemed to have been killed. The man who had been shot through a window was suffering badly, and I and others took turns to sit with him. Eventually stretchers arrived from headquarters and we were able to send him and a few others back; also the prisoners and the wounded German who had been in the farm buildings at the back. The stretcher bearers told us of the disaster to the reinforcements who had walked into the minefield; but extra ammunition had got through, although no food, and we had eaten nothing since sodden sandwiches the previous midday. Someone found me a bit of black German bread which I ate ravenously.

There remained the question of what we would find outside in the morning. There had been a lot of distant firing and explosions and tracers from the hills during the night: presumably the large-scale attack on Spaduro had gone in, but to what effect we could not tell. If it had failed we would be under exposed siege for another whole day. Desmond had set about building up protective rubble in the doors and windows. I seemed to be both too tired and too triumphant to care. Whatever had been attempted, or destined, or hoped for, had come off: and I did not think anything else could really fail.

At first light we were standing to and looking out into the cold mist like people in a Western film wondering if they would see Red Indians or the Cavalry. There were figures moving on the further hills: surely they were acting too openly to be enemy? We risked a small cheer. After a while it seemed safe to step out of the front of the house into the space where only a few hours ago there had been such danger: there were some bodies of Germans lying about, one of them blocking the opening into the dug-out on the right. We pulled this clear; there was still no sight or sound of anyone inside. I called in my best German again for people to come out; and then to our surprise there emerged, one by one, like wasps from a hole, twelve men, about half of them wounded. We had not expected so many.

We sent them back under escort. The second-in-command of our company came up to take over arrangements for further defence; our battalion commander came up to congratulate us, and said that the night attack on Spaduro had been a success, thanks in a large part to the success of our attack on Spinello. We hung about for the rest of the day while the situation in the hills became clearer. We were told to dig trenches outside the farm-house in case the shelling started again, but no one paid much attention. In the evening we set about marching back – not just to our previous positions but to somewhere near Castel del Rio where we could rest. But this was a long march, and I and others were suffering both from exhaustion and a reaction of extreme otherworldliness. During a ten-minute rest on the march an officer who had not been in the battle came along the line and told us to get up and get a move on. I remember telling him to fuck off.

I wrote a long account of this battle to be sent some time later to my sister; and it is from this, as well as memory, that I have taken many of the details of this account. I ended my letter by saying 'I find it hard to believe it was I that did all those peculiar things!' and then as if in an attempt at explanation – 'I have yet to meet a man who fought well because he believes in the cause for which he is fighting . . . it is always pride that incites and succeeds in war.'

9

The war in Europe lasted another seven months. I did not get home for almost another year. After the battle of Casa Spinello, war became a matter of sticking it out; not something of which the outcome was in much doubt. Spaduro had been taken; but we still did not get through to the plain that autumn. There was too much rain, our forces were too depleted. For myself, I had done what I had wanted to do at Spinello – or what had been required, or destined. Now I wanted to get home. Pride may be required if a human feels he has to perform some task; after that it makes sense no longer.

The battalion stayed in the northern hills until well into the new year. There were more waterlogged trenches, more farm-yards with rotting cattle; but no more attacks that winter. Daily existence became largely a matter of chores – weapons testing and inspection, the digging of latrines, the official inspection of feet – foot-rot had become a prevalent but preventable disease. Every so often we went down for a few days rest to tents in the valley. I huddled under blankets and tried to read.

The canister of books I had brought with me from England had got lost somewhere on my travels in the summer: then it turned up as if miraculously on my return from Egypt. I came across an officer whom I did not know reading, of all things, a book by Richard Jefferies: I asked him how he had come across it. He said that a strange box had turned up in his luggage that looked as if it should contain ammunition, but then – Well, he was extraordinarily grateful to me because he had been enjoying stuff that he would otherwise not have read; but of course I must have the canister back.

But now, in the mountains in the rain, I had run out of books: and anyway I did not know what I wanted to read. The world seemed so mad: did art, literature, make it any better? However somewhere on our journey to the north we had stayed near a recently liberated prisoner-of-war camp which had a Red Cross library of English books; and we had been told we could pick out and keep any we liked. I had chosen a book by William Faulkner, of whom I had not heard, but it had an introduction by Richard Hughes whom I admired. So I now read *The Sound and the Fury* in a bivouac tent in the pouring rain; conditions were too wet almost literally to put it down. Much of the story is told by a mentally defective youth who hardly tries to make sense of the world around him; sense has to be looked for, hoped for, by the reader. There are flashbacks, narrations by other members of the family, in the course of which there are glimpses of things becoming clearer; then about two thirds of the way through the whole import of the story, its structure and meaning, burst upon the reader in a flash. I had never come across anything like this before. I thought – Yes this is how life may be understood, if at all: this is the way in which I want to write novels after the war.

Mervyn had been carried off to hospital after Spinello. I had a letter from him from Arezzo.

> Dear Nick, I have been thinking a great deal about you lately, which goes without saying. I was so glad to see Mann the signaller chap who said you were safe enough and coming out of the line for a bit. I hope it is for a long time. This letter is really to get you to write some account of what happened after I left. I will not hold forth in a long and boring screed myself because I cannot write very well my left arm being in a sling. I am well enough and I suppose will be in bed for about a fortnight. Your performance at Casa Spinello was great. I told the C.O. and the rough draft of a recommendation I sent from the hospital is with this letter. I was very fed up with myself at the Casa. I reckon myself pretty good in battle, but my performance there was the worst ever. It was certainly your greatest ever but anyway we had better not begin such a discussion by post. Pray write. Love to Fitz, Desmond and Co. Yours, Mervyn.

It had not seemed to anyone else that Mervyn's performance at Spinello had not been great. He too had been recommended for an award, as had Desmond; and Corporals Tomkinson and McClarnon on my recommendation. Because the battle of Spinello had been such an important one for the whole division, it had been watched by the Brigadier and the 78th Division General through binoculars from a vantage point on a distant hill. So its fame had spread.

We were not out of the line for as long as Mervyn had hoped; and then there were night patrols again – and these were not always now an uneventful game. There was one position where we were separated from the Germans by a shallow valley along which a road ran between us and them; half-way along this road there was a bridge over a small river. It was not feasible for either us or the Germans to occupy this bridge during the day; but for some military reason it was considered crucial by both sides to be in possession of it at night. So every evening at dusk there was a race to see who would get to the bridge first: if we started too early we got shot up by the Germans in the light; if we started too late we got shot up in the dark by Germans who had got there first. At regular intervals it came to be the turn of my platoon to do this race. This was the sort of nerve-racking routine that made people break down during this long and wearying winter. There were in fact one or two officers who said they could not go on. This was understood by higher authority; they were not persecuted as they would have been in the First World War; they were sent back to jobs at the base. Any fear of this leading to a spate of such occurrences did not materialise. If one had not had pride, one would not have been in the front line anyway.

From one of our positions I wrote to my father –

I have constructed for myself a pleasantly secluded little dungeon in the rubble of a ruined house, about 7 ft. by 5 ft. and 3 ft. high, in which I hibernate for

24 hours a day, passing the time happily in commun-
ing with the less lofty Muses, concocting grotesque
dishes of tinned food to fry over a tiny petrol fire, and
beating off the savage assaults of many rats who share
my compartment. For a limited period I am strangely
content to exist thus. Unfortunately the higher Muses
cannot be invoked because one has not yet achieved
the degree of detachment whereby the inquiring mind
can free itself from bodily squalor.

But then from the luxury of a tent in the valley –

Have been reading quite a lot of Shakespeare and Ibsen
– food for interesting comparison. But it seems to me
that the greatness of both as artists depends on the
fact that they are neither of them profound or ardent
philosophers. Thus they produce art for art's sake;
even Ibsen, who is careful in his plays never to solve
the problems he presents; or if he does, to contra-
dict his first solution in a later play, thus using social,
moral and spiritual problems merely as a framework
for his art. This leads me to wonder if philosophy
and perfect art can ever be reconciled. In Goethe,
perhaps you would say? But that is a subject I know
little about.

I was still dreaming about possibilities for life after the
war. For so long even before the war the family had been split
– with my father, my stepmother and my half-brothers in their

beautiful house in Derbyshire; my sister, brother and Nanny in my mother's old home at Denham, Bucks, under the eye of my aunt Irene – and myself happy to move between the two. Then at the start of the war the Derbyshire house had been relinquished, the house at Denham had been requisitioned by some hush-hush scientific establishment, and my brother Micky and Nanny had gone to stay with my other aunt Baba in Gloucestershire. Now my father and Diana were settled into a new house and – and what? It seemed that only I thought it feasible that we should all get together again. Eventually I wrote to my sister – 'If Daddy does not want to accept the Micky guardianship of course it puts everything in a different light. I totally agree with you that we must not forget the old Aunt Nina-Nanny ties, and if, as you say, we cannot combine them with the Daddy ties, they must be kept separate but intact.'

And as if to assure each other of the sanctity of old child-hood ties, when I came to give my sister a first intimation of the battle of Casa Spinello, in order to divert the attention of the censor I described it as if it had been one of our children's games.

I have been playing the Cornwall game with a bunch of the most energetic Germans, who defended their base with distressing determination. However it was the long run round the kitchen garden that did it in the end, and the crafty lurk on top of the garden wall; and then we were into the swimming-pool area, too close for sight, and the poor dears are not very good when it comes to touch. But serioso, the

lionesque games are an excellent training for this sort
of life. We had a little skirmish around a farmhouse,
the success of which I attribute very largely to my
ability to leap over staircases, vanish into lavatories,
and come crashing through the plaster of a roof.

And then, when we got to the place where there was the race
each night to the bridge over the river –

I find that lions in the open with the Germans is not
nearly so exhilarating as lions in the house. In fact it is
pure hell. I am at the moment horribly war-weary and
longing for a little wound in the arm again.

I was granted four days' leave in Florence. I remember little
of this my first visit to Florence except that the museums and
galleries were closed with their works of arts in crates in the
cellars. So the beautiful buildings had more than ever the air of
fortresses; of a town fashioned by war; the home of the Medicis
and Savonarola. But then – was it not true that great art had
been produced in time of war – when people had been in daily
confrontation with danger and death; with extremes of evil and
sanctity? In my memory, the statues of Michelangelo's *David* and
Cellini's *Perseus* were still on show in the Square. Or these must
have been copies? I remember absurdly bribing my way into the
locked Bargello Museum and in the basement staring at a crate
that was said to contain Donatello's *David*.

I had another letter from Mervyn who was now in hospital in
Rome. He was distressed to hear that the reinforcements he had

asked to be sent up to Spinello had walked into the minefield, and
that their company commander Ronnie Boyd had been killed.

> Dear Nick, I feel in a frantic letter-writing mood so I
> am going to set about you. I have been lying in bed (in
> many hospitals, in many places) and saying to myself
> everyday – now you must do something more than
> reading *Esquire* and get on to reading something in-
> tense like Nietzsche; and writing copious notebooks
> which no one will ever read except yourself. But every
> day has been just the same, and I still stare weakly at
> *Esquire* different copies of which appear from I don't
> know where.
>
> I'm still worried over that Ronnie Boyd business
> for I told the C.O. to send F Company along that way,
> having travelled it myself.
>
> I met a Rifle Brigade subaltern on my way down: I
> forget his name, but he asked after you. Typical R.B.,
> because he evidently regarded you as eccentric in
> staying away from the R.B. which to him, he made
> plain, was the most satisfactory regiment one could
> ever be in. He was very nice.
>
> This leg of mine is getting on well, but they keep
> messing around with my arm, and I gather are going
> to do a third operation on it. Myself I think there is
> nothing wrong with it, I'm afraid.
>
> I am so glad to have remembered to tell you that
> the Penguin Shakespeares must be avoided. I had
> been reading *Hamlet* off and on for months from the

normal version in that American book I had. In hospital I picked up a Penguin *Hamlet* and the difference is distressing. Nearly as bad as reading the Bible R.V. after being used to the A.V.

I must try to get a few books while in this place for it was so enjoyable to argue about T. Mann and so on, and to discover that you were a Hellenist pagan and that I was a puritan more than I realised. I must get you weaving on Tolstoy – myself too, for I have not really worked him out. Did you finish *Resurrection*? It was horribly translated but the simplicity of the ideas that the chap arrived at were very impressive. Neklyadoff I think he was called. I love these Russian names.

Good luck and learn to go carefully. No heroics. Yours, Mervyn.

As Christmas approached we were in a quieter part of the line and the weather cleared. There was a slope to a valley below and no sign of Germans; we could once more sit and admire the beautiful landscape. There was a farmstead in the valley that seemed deserted – except for a pig or two that snuffled about and a gaggle of strutting turkeys. We eyed these greedily. As soon as we were out of danger we were aware of hunger. It occurred to me and I think to all my platoon that for once a really sensible patrol would be to go down into the valley and take prisoner a few turkeys. One of my men claimed to have been in civilian life a butcher; he said that if we escorted him to the farmyard he would dispatch a few of them quickly and silently.

So we set off, just before dusk, fully armed, five or six of us; and we proceeded peacefully into the valley. We surrounded the hut where we had watched the turkeys go to roost; the self-designated butcher crept in with a bayonet. After a moment the hut exploded as if a grenade had gone off inside; turkeys flew squawking and flapping in all directions, the man with the bayonet in pursuit of them vainly. Someone shouted – Shoot them! I shouted – No! Eventually we managed to capture a few: we carried them back in triumph, and had our pre-Christmas dinner.

I had a letter from Mervyn –

> It is fortunate that there is a brandy allocation in the ward as I really had to call for it after reaching your demoniac denunciation of *Resurrection* and your relegation of it to the futile and obvious. I have certainly got over my first rapture on its account, but I really do regard it as frightfully interesting account of the working of God (or what one pleases to put in place of that word) on a man's mind. It is certainly not original, as you say, but it does describe how a wrongful act worries the mind until at last you feel you have to do something to make up for it. As I understand them, Tolstoy and Dostoievsky regard this as the direct influence of God. I think (with respect) that you miss the point of the last chapter on the Sermon on the Mount. That is added as a personal reflection of the author and is not really concerned with the story at all. It was his last book and I feel he could

not quite confine himself to a dissection of the mind of le bon Neklyadov but kept breaking into his own theological thoughts.

Really of course why we disagree is as plain to you as it is to me. You can look at the efforts of a man to convince one of Christianity in a detached fashion and can be critical both of Christianity and his ways. I, on the other hand, am so desperately anxious to be convinced of Christianity's truth that I am unable to look with that critical Mosley eye. So I suppose you will call me a bigoted old puritan and smile at your own openmindedness – with satisfaction of course.

There is just one other thing you say that I must comment on, to disagree again I am afraid. You say men will not follow the Sermon on the Mount until they are sane and merciful, and when they are that it does not matter what sermon (creed) they punch up. Apart from the fact that the second part of your conclusion implicitly denies that Jesus is of God, I reckon that the first conclusion is wrong because chaps will become sane and merciful by practising the Sermon and not, as you say, will practise the Sermon when they are S. and M. The Sermon is the means pointed out to men whereby they can better the world; and this means will end in folks being good and kind, or sane and merciful.

Then there came a day in the New Year when we were in the mountains again – somewhere close to Monte Spaduro I think – and the weather was still fine and there was no sign of Germans; and I was standing beside my trench in the sunlight and I saw our Commanding Officer, Bala Bredin, and his adjutant coming along a path up the hill; and they were moving in a stately manner like a small religious procession and smiling; and I thought – So that is all right. And then Bala came up to me and said that for the battle of Casa Spinello I had been awarded the Military Cross; and so had Mervyn; and Desmond Fay had got a bar to the MC he already had; and Corporal Tomkinson had got a Military Medal and Corporal McClarnon had been Mentioned in Despatches. And so what I had not exactly hoped for nor expected but had felt I needed – this had happened; and perhaps I would not have to feel cynical again.

Mervyn wrote –

> I was vastly pleased to get your letter and to read that we have both been begonged and Desmond has been bebarred. My salutations to you (and D.) and thanks for yours. I will not go on with any more mutual admiration except to say that I reckon we are all mighty fine fellows!
>
> I knew yours was coming of course because the C.O. told me in a letter. Your mighty charge was terrific to see.

I wrote to my sister –

> It's the full ridicule, the ultimate absurdity, but there it is – a slender little purple and while ribbon stitched

upon my heaving bosom, and me in the full enjoyment of outrageous false modesty.

   The MC will help, yes, for it will give authority to
the anti-war, anti-patriotic preaching which I intend
to deliver to one and all after the war. Even in this
so-called universal war there are so very few people
who have seen anything of the real fighting, that it is
essential for these few to bellow their views even if
it means discomforting others. I hope you won't find
me too soap-boxish and bitter.

To my father I wrote –

It is the young Siegfried after all.

10

The superficial aspect of elation did not last long. We were soon
back at the place we had so disliked a month or so ago – with
the race to the bridge across the stream. More people were now
saying they could not go on.

I had one man in my platoon – an ex-jail-bird from Belfast
– who was known as a trouble-maker; in army jargon a barrack-
room lawyer. I made him my batman/runner because I thought
he would be less trouble under my eye than away from it. He
was also an invigorating 'character.' Once when we were in our
perilous position by the bridge I ordered him to take a message
back to headquarters, and he refused. I said 'Obey my order or
I shall shoot you!' He said 'Then shoot me sir!' – and tore open
the front of his battledress. I said 'Oh all right!'

I arranged a new nook for myself on the first floor of a hayloft;
it was exposed to the shelling, but away from the attention of
rats. I began to fantasise about how one might get out of this
futile situation by a discreet self-inflicted accident: would this be
more or less reprehensible now that I had got an MC? I imagined

I might fall from my hayloft on to the concrete floor below with one leg tucked under the other in a yoga position: might this not give me a not-too-badly broken leg which would get me back to hospital? But after a time luck was once more with me. I awoke one morning shivering and sweating with something other than fear; the Medical Officer confirmed I had a high temperature, and diagnosed malaria. So off I went in an ambulance bumping painfully over pot-holed roads, but how happy to be on a magical mystery tour again to – where – Florence? Rome? even Naples?

I wrote to my sister from Florence –

> Jan 13th. I have malaria, or at least I am told I have by the learned doctors who prod my stomach. I maintain it is jaundice, and contest them every inch of the way, but they continue to pump me with quinine until I am stone deaf and sick every three minutes. I have not even the consolation of being unexpectedly out of the line – for just before I left had been offered a fearfully smart job for 2 months at the Div. Training School, where I would have been a Captain and reasonably comfortable.
>
> Jan 14th. I have triumphed over the forces of science. It is jaundice, which apparently is treated far more seriously, and I am to be evacuated back, and the further back the happier I shall be. I don't know if I shall quite make Naples, but I should drift as far as Rome.

But then I did go all the way to Naples, and then on to a convalescent home in Sorrento, which as it happened was next door to the hotel in which I had stayed with my father and sister and stepmother in 1936. In hospital and on my journeys down I had been thinking – If ever in later life I come to write about all this I must try to find a style in which to express the contradictions of war – the coincidence of luck and endurance; of farce and fear; of anarchy and meaning.

From Sorrento I wrote to my sister a long letter in which I tried to say what I thought I had learned from war. The direction of my arrogance had somewhat changed, but did not seem to be done away with.

I wrote –

I went into this war with certain pompous opinions about my virtues and capabilities but amongst them were absolutely no pretensions that I would make a good soldier. I thought that all business-minded men would be 100 times better at organisation than myself, and I thought that all the earnest hearties who serious-ly believed in the righteousness of this war would be 100 times more brave. After twelve months in Italy I realised that I was wrong: I did not under-estimate my own abilities; I overestimated almost everyone else's. And this startles me considerably; for I, as you know, consider this war a blasphemous stupidity, and yet in a spirit of unwilling desperation I have put more into the winning of it than most of those who say they consider it a holy crusade against the powers of the Devil.

I still do not think I have any pretensions about myself as a soldier. When things are not dangerously active I am intensely and professedly idle. Every minute I have to give to this war I grudge angrily. And when things are dangerously active I go about my business in a spirit of complete misery. And yet I have the reputation of being in action a model subaltern.

It is interesting to note that after 12 months of fighting I will forgive anyone the old failings – the boorishness, the stupidity, the dullness – if he does not possess the failings of a bad soldier. That boils down to the realisation that out here the only thing that matters tuppence in a man is his ability to be brave. That is the only standard by which one judges anyone. For if they are not brave, it is 10 to 1 that they are miserably hypocritical as well.

Now there are incredibly few people who do possess this virtue. Those who possess it least are those who preach most lustily about the holiness of the war crusade. Fortunately in my battalion nearly everyone does possess it: they do not remain long if they don't; and that is why I am able to get on very well with them, whereas before I would have been driven into my frenzy of petulance by their shortcomings. But this breeds tolerance for people who are fundamentally worthy. The war is a head-sweller to the few who fight it; but it produces a lofty, cynical, benign swollen head – which does not rant or strut but maintains an almost reverent humility towards anyone who knows why and whereof it is swollen. So when you see me although you may find me complacent I hope it does not take too odious a form. On the whole I think the tolerance and humility with those who understand will be far more prominent than the other feelings. But you will find out!

I tried to explain to my sister the origins of my feeling an outsider. My sister and I had been very close as children: with both our parents so often away (my mother as well as my father had been for four years a Labour MP) we had come to depend on each other; we told each fantasy stories in which we were literally orphans in a storm – marooned on a desert island or on a raft. My sister dealt with our situation with considerable boldness if not confidence; I was likely to get in desperate rages and try to hide myself away. Now my sister wrote to me that our brother Michael, aged twelve, was behaving in much the same way as I had done; and what should she do? In the same long letter in which I wrote to her about myself in the war, I wrote about what it seemed that such a child has to contend with.

The trouble begins when a child (or youth or what-have-you) has a constructively vivid imagination, an intolerant but quick mind, and a sensitive but intense-ly self-centred nature. Which is what I had and Mick has. So soon as such a child begins to think he will form certain ideas in his imagination which are made very strong and definite by the quickness and intoler-ance of his mind, and are very real to him owing to the virulence of his imagination. The most important of these ideas, owing to his self-centred nature, will be his ideas of himself and of how things and people ought to behave in relation to himself. Gradually as these ideas grow in clarity, and his sensitiveness and intolerance grow in intensity, he will have an increasing horror of anything that does not conform to these ideas, a horror which in some exaggerated cases becomes almost physical. Thus when he is faced with conditions which are antipathetic to his ideas, his revolt against them is spontaneous and unavoidable. In his revolt he can do one of two things. He can either try to change the conditions or he must run from them. But a child cannot change his conditions because he is neither strong enough nor has a definite enough idea what to change them to. So he sulks. He runs away. It is an almost physical reaction.

Does this explain my behaviour? I did not understand it at the time. All I knew was that in certain conditions I reacted in a way which I really could not control. I am not very clear even now as to what those conditions were, but you will remember the numerous examples as well as I. I think 'artificiality' and 'unpleasantness' were the chief characteristics of the conditions I abhorred. But these are vague terms, and it is fruitless to try to analyse them accurately. And the 'artificiality' or 'unpleasantness' was always relative only to me. Viewed dispassionately, there was very often nothing objectionable in the conditions at all. It was all a matter of how they acted on my frame of mind at the moment.

I wrote briefly and not analytically about my stammer –

On the surface I suppose it is a tragedy. Certainly without it I should have shone much more than I did at Eton. Even in the army it probably stops me from promotion. But the stammer forced me away from all superficial contacts, from all superficialities in fact. And although on the face of it this was unfortunate and forbade much material 'success,' I am presumptuous enough to feel that it led to many developments in a more fundamental way. It taught me to think and to judge, to see things at more than their superficial values; to rely on more than affability to show my worth. If the stammer eventually goes, I am convinced it will have done me more good than harm. If it stays, at least it will have been of some advantage early in life, when I might so easily have become a vacant lout. I think myself it will go in time.

After Sorrento I found myself once more in what I described to my sister as 'the full gaiety of the Naples winter season.' When I had reported back this time to the Transit camp to learn what arrangements would be made to get me back to the battalion they told me that they had no papers about me and would be able to do nothing with me until they had. This seemed to have something to do with the uncertainly about my being classified as either London Irish Rifles or Rifle Brigade, or neither. This situation of course I felt suited me very well – not just now, in Naples, but in my feeling that I was by nature an outsider – not tied to any group. So I was encouraged by the authorities again to go off on my own, with this time no indication about when

I should come back. It was too cold and wet to go to Ischia or Capri, so I set about looking for a room in the old part of Naples, by the harbour, where from tall buildings washing like flags was hung across narrow streets. This was the haunt of touts who would offer soldiers their 'virgin' sisters in return for cigarettes. I soon found a man who said he could find me a splendid apartment in return for very little money. So I was taken to a high unprepossessing building and up bleak flights of stairs to the home of an elderly and kind couple who showed me two beautifully furnished rooms which they said I could rent. So I moved in with my meagre kit-bag, and sat on an antique sofa beneath an ornate gilded mirror, and I thought – This is the first place truly of my own that I have ever had: it gives rise to a form of ecstasy.

I took up again my correspondence with my father that seemed to represent a sanity-seeking journey in contrast to that of war.

Have just read the most enthralling little book called *The Mysterious Universe* by James Jeans. It appears that the physicists have indeed done away with the old theories of matter and energy, and have arrived by scientific means at much the same conclusions that Berkeley and Co hazarded in the 18th century. The point I find fascinating is the scientific conclusion that the universe as we know it cannot be composed of ultimate matter and energy, but only the reflections of ultimate reality in some Universal Mind. And we are only able to see these reflections as reflections again in our own mind. Now this is a very acceptable conclusion when it is come by scientifically, for although

the Universal Mind seems to be the mind of a Pure
Mathematician, and thus forever somewhat beyond
our comprehension, it does at least suggest that the
Universal Mind has some affinity with our own feeble
minds, thus giving us enormous significance in the
universe when before it seemed as if we were of no
account at all.

And later —

Before I came into contact with the physicists I had
embarked on a rather dangerous heresy reasoning as
follows: — Although we admit the hypothetical existence of God and Ultimate Reality, it appears that
both are so irrevocably incomprehensible to us that
there is no way by which man can approach them:
Ultimate Reality is eternally indiscernible, and there
is no reason to suppose that the will, intelligence or
purpose of God is anywhere manifested upon earth,
either in mankind or 'nature.' Why do we suppose
that we have in us that which is also in God?

Reasoning thus, without the evidence of the physicists, I evolved a 'man for man's sake' religion, the only
ethics of which were those imposed by the conscience
of the individual — a religion close to that of the terrible Friedrich! [Nietzsche] Without the physicists'
evidence I think that was a reasonable view; but after
my introduction to Jeans, I saw that there were very
good grounds for the belief that 'we have in us that

which is also in God': also that the natural world is in some way a reflection of eternal reality. However, in either philosophy our attitude to life can be much the same – the aim being always the perfecting of man and a possible creation of a higher type of man. Whether this is the end in itself – as it was with N – or merely the means whereby we may ultimately come in contact with Reality or Godhead, does not greatly matter. We shall doubtless know when the time comes. In the meantime to the sane man there can be only attitude to life – to find a harmony between his consciousness and his instinct by a study of the world about him and the world that has gone before him, and an honest appreciation of the evidence thereby attained – and then to live in accordance with this harmony, always with the further purpose of increasing its range and imparting it to others. If ever a fairly universal harmony is obtained, a higher type of man will emerge. So long as the ignorant and prejudiced are in the vast majority, the harmonious man has to devote most of his energy to shielding himself from the insane clamour of the multitude; but if ever sanity is able to extend itself from the individual to society, then indeed I think there will be hope of higher creation.

This particular would-be harmonious man continued on his way through a Naples winter. My old friend Anthony, back in Italy after having been treated for his wound in England, sought me out in the convalescent home and later came to stay with me in my flat. We went to the opera – *Carmen*, *La Boheme*, *Faust*, *Turandot*, *La Traviata*. Gigli and Maria Caniglia were said to be expected from Rome. We visited Herculaneum and Pompei; we climbed Vesuvius. In the Officers' Club we got drunk and belted out Neapolitan songs to the accompaniment of a rousing band, or swayed to sentimental yearnings about St Lucia or return to Sorrento. Occasionally there were a few nurses at the club, and I remember going with one for a moonlit walk by the sea. But as I had found in Cairo – sex did not seem to have much point in war; unless, that is, one had something of the nature of a rapist.

My friend from Ranby days, Raleigh Trevelyan, who had been badly wounded at Anzio, was now working for the Military Mission to the Italian Army in Rome, where the social life was more glamorous, and he suggested I should join him. He wrote – 'I exchange pleasantries with Marchesas and dance on polished floors to the gramophone with Ambassadors' daughters; every Friday I partake of tea and scones with the Princess Doria . . . the Vestal Virgins are preparing a bullock, snow white, to sacrifice in your honour; the priests of Dionysus are already weaving garlands to adorn the pillars of the temple.' This was the old Ranby style of which I had been so fond and which I had got out of the way of with the London Irish Rifles. Later, Raleigh wrote – 'How unfashionable you are supporting Gigli! You'll be a social failure in Rome.'

I still had nostalgia for the Rifle Brigade style, although I had not wanted to go back to it. When Mervyn had been convalescing in Sorrento earlier in the year and I was still laid up in

Florence, he had bumped into Anthony and they had got on so well together that they had hatched a plot for Anthony to join the LIR. So when Mervyn got back to the battalion at the end of January 1945 – just as I arrived in Naples – he had spoken of this plan to our Commanding Officer, who had welcomed the idea, and had had a word with so-and-so who had had a word – and so on – and everything seemed to be in train for Anthony to join us until the Rifle Brigade got fed up and scotched the idea. In the meantime however Mervyn seemed to have become imbued with something of the old Ranby style, and we wrote to each other about forming, with or without Anthony, a society of like-minded refugees from the earnest gung-ho spirit of war, to be known as the SDA or the Society of Decadent Anarchists. My two or three great friends and I already saw ourselves as forming what we referred to as a clique which felt itself aloof from conventional society; which made jokes about our current predicaments, and talked seriously about the meaning of life and God.

But now, owing to the non-existence of papers about me, there seemed some doubt about my getting back into the war at all. I cannot remember the details of this: it seems so unlikely! I gather what I can from Mervyn's letters. It appears that I really might have been free to go on doing as I wished – even to stay on indefinitely in my Naples flat. But then – might I not seriously be in some limbo for ever? A sort of non-person unable to get home? Mervyn wrote from the batallion who were now on the edge of the northern plain – 'What I really want you to know is that you will not be sailing up the creek if you come here under your own steam.' That is, the battalion would then sort things out. Mervyn spoke of huge St Patrick's Day parties being planned. I thought – Surely there is no point in being an outsider unless one also has the choice of being an insider?

So I set off on my own to rejoin the 2nd LIR towards the end of March. I by-passed Raleigh in Rome. I arrived at Forli on the edge of the plain, where the battalion were getting ready to celebrate a postponed St Patrick's Day because on the proper day, March 17th, they had still been in the line. The winter break-through had never quite been achieved, but I was regaled with hair-raising stories of the latest battles on the banks of the canals and rivers that criss-crossed the eastern end of the Po valley. But I was glad to be back in the battalion; to be with people with whom I had been through so much already. I wrote to my father –

> I still wonder at my good fortune at having found my way to this battalion. The Rifle Brigade was all very jolly in the insouciant days of Winchester and York, but out here I think I would have been stifled by their so carefully posed artificiality of decency. Here the atmosphere is almost Dionysian.
>
> When I went away in January I left behind my little translation of *Zarathustra*, with earnest instructions to one and all that they should read it before I came back. I find that they have followed my instructions to such good effect that the talk that floats around the Mess at dinner time is not of obscenities or military pomposities to which one might have become resigned, but is full of erudite allusions to Will to

Power, Superman, Feast of the Ass, etc; which, although no one knows very well what he is talking about, I find most comforting. It is surely unique to find the Mess of an infantry battalion that discusses *Zarathustra*?

On the postponed St Patrick's Day we all got uproariously drunk. Anthony joined us briefly on his way to joining a battalion of the King's Royal Rifle Corps. The London Irish were due to set off in a day or two on what at last could reasonably be hoped to be the final battle of the Italian campaign. We were all lined up for inspection before setting off when my batman, the one who had invited me to shoot him for refusing to obey an order, was seen to be swaying alarmingly. The Brigadier stopped in front of him and said 'What's wrong with you my good man?' My batman said 'Sir, I'm drunk.'

This was now the second week in April 1945. For the advance across the promised land of the Po Valley and the northern plain we were for the first time since Cassino a year ago going to work with tanks and the support of heavy artillery; also now there would be fighter-bombers overhead ready to be called up to deal with opposition if it became serious. The tank regiment we were going to work with was the fashionable 9th Lancers, with two or three of whose officers I had been at school. We eyed one another warily: what on earth was I doing with the London Irish Rifles? Once I would have thought – But I'm not 'with' anyone: now I was rather pleased to be seen as being Allied to something unfashionable.

The Irish Brigade was set to advance through something called the Argenta Gap – a stretch of artificially drained land at the eastern end of the Po Valley which lay between areas that had been flooded. The Fusiliers and Inniskillings were to make the initial breakthrough across the Senio and Santerno rivers; then the London Irish were to exploit this, working in teams with tanks – one troop of tanks to each platoon. The infantry were to be carried in armoured personnel carriers known as Kangaroos – three to a platoon – consisting of the bodies of tanks or self-propelled guns with the turrets or armaments removed. When the going was straightforward the tanks would go ahead and be in charge; when they came across anti-tank opposition they would stop and give covering fire while the infantry dismounted and took charge and did a text-book attack on foot. With luck, we were told, the enemy would surrender.

This was my first experience of what might be called the heroic aspect of war – the sort of thing Germans must have experienced in Poland and France in 1939 and 1940 and in the earliest days of the Russian campaign – tanks rolling across flat country and people emerging with their hands up and what little opposition there was being dive-bombed while those in tanks could watch as if at an air show. Here in Italy people came out from villages and farmsteads with flowers and bottles of wine and the offer of kisses. In the fields there was the occasional German tank now burning and with a body perhaps hanging like a rag doll from the turret.

It was not of course always like this. Once a neighbouring Kangaroo was hit by an anti-tank shell and the people in my carrier were showered with bits of blood and bone. Then there were the times when we were on foot again and doing our training-ground attacks – 'One and two sections round on the right, three section give covering fire!' But more often than not, yes, when we got to our objective the enemy had disappeared. With us gaining in confidence I could even try out a more democratic form of leadership, about the feasibility of which I had wondered. Once when the tanks had been held up by some anti-tank fire from a farmstead and I had ordered – 'Dismount! We'll go round by that ditch' – a voice from my platoon piped up – 'Sir, wouldn't it be better if we went round in the carriers as far as that clump of trees and then dismounted?' And I saw the sense of this, so I shouted – 'You're absolutely right! Everyone back in the carriers!' And by the time we eventually got to our objective the enemy was indeed pulling out. My platoon seemed to appreciate this readiness to change one's mind; though it would probably only have worked in a war as good as won.

There was a constant problem with prisoners. As we advanced from Argenta towards Ferrara more and more Germans were waiting for us with their hands up. We could not easily spare the men to escort them back; yet the time had not come when we could leave them to their own devices. On the second or third day of our advance the tank major who was nominally in command of our Infantry platoon told us, when giving out his daily orders, that we were taking too many prisoners. He repeated – Did we understand? We were taking too many prisoners. One of us, probably Desmond Fay, quietly spat on the ground. And we went on taking too many prisoners.

In Richard Doherty's *History of the Irish Brigade* the story of this advance is one of strategies and deployments of forces – this many regiments of field artillery here; that number of specially equipped tanks for crossing ditches and clearing mines there; such and such squadrons of planes on call overhead in what was called a 'cab-rank.' The plans and orders were precise: also what could be said to have succeeded and what could not.

But there was not much need to talk of failure. Instead there were statistics – the Irish Brigade had taken prisoner '22 officers and 2000 other ranks'; casualties inflicted had been 'far greater'; 'seven mark IV German tanks were knocked out by the 9th Lancers for the loss of only one of their own.' From what I could see I did not think that there were many casualties on either side: certainly not on our own, apart from those in the carrier that had been hit. But what stays in my memory, as at Cassino, was the impression that no individual could know much of what was going on; one had to wait and see when it was over. But here it could be felt indeed that things were going well: and I began to feel I understood something of what those ghastly Nazi armies must have felt as they bludgeoned their way smiling across Poland, France, Russia; until nemesis caught up with them and the homes they had left behind were utterly flattened, and there was no heroic ideology for them to come back to. I wrote to my father –

> It is a happier form of warfare than any we have done before, but I find it exhibits the most unfortunate characteristics of one's nature. I actually find this conquest and pursuit faintly enjoyable – and at last understand the fatal temptation of aggression. But nevertheless it is for the most part tedious, and I am irked by the feeling that the end ever remains the same distance from us even as we advance.

However there came a day early in May when we were on the outskirts of Ferrara and the crowds coming out with flowers were even more ebullient than usual, and the bangs and whooshes that could be heard were of fireworks rather than grenades or Moaning Minnies; and the German trenches we were occupying were deserted except for a litter of old love-letters and a smell of stale bread. And the German radio was playing Wagner – the "Entry of the Gods into Valhalla" I think – and it dawned on us that our war was over. Some of those I was with said later that they almost immediately began to feel strangely at a loss: for so long the war had provided a structure for their lives; a means of getting on with things in spite of doubts and fears. This feeling seemed to persist. However I took the opportunity to borrow a jeep and drive into Ferrara to have a look at its 14th-century castle – a massive turreted building with reddish walls and a moat with drawbridges. This was a monument to war now to be preserved for tourists. And as an adjunct to triumphalism, there was now the promise of loot.

When the Germans began to surrender en masse on the 2nd of May and were rounded up and carted off to prison camps they had to leave behind – everything. The sides of the roads were littered with both the large-scale and the personal detritus of war – tanks, trucks, heavy guns; but also, in piles, abandoned personal weapons and possessions. We searched through these for what trophies we might pick out – in particular the prized Luger pistol. I took my fill of pistols and even a shotgun or two; and then I came across a small and pretty piano accordion – on which quite soon I learnt to play the rousing and sentimental Neapolitan songs that had seemed so much part of our war. Also one's platoon could now be fitted out with its own means of transport. I wrote to my sister –

Kennen Sie what victory means? It means I am at the
moment the tempestuous possessor of three cars – a
Mercedes which goes at such a horrific speed that I
am terrified to take it beyond second gear; an Adler
saloon which cruises at 60 without the slightest indication that it is moving; an Opel which streaks hither
and thither to the desperate confusion of stray pe-
destrians. It means that we dine on champagne each
night except when we feel leery enough to start on
the brandy with the soup. It means – oh well, so much
really beyond cars and wine that I suppose they are of
infinitesimal significance.

The army was tolerant about such loot. Someone had to clear
up the personal stuff by the road, and for a time we were allowed to keep the cars because transport was needed to get us
to Austria – or to Yugoslavia, or wherever we were now heading.
Rumours abounded; there were few official briefings. In Austria
we might be needed to get to somewhere or other ahead of the
Russians who were advancing apace from the east; for although
the Russians had been our much-lauded allies during the war, we
didn't actually trust them, did we? (What – they might carry on
marching west with their vast armies till they reached the Chan-
nel ports?) About Yugoslavia the briefings were as confusing as
the rumours. We had been backing Marshal Tito who had been
fighting a guerrilla war for years against the occupying Germans;
but Tito was a communist, and he would surely now be aligning
himself with the Russians. Also he was a Serbian, and might well
take the opportunity to annihilate his traditional enemies the

Croatians, who had tended to side with the Germans. But the Croatians were trying to surrender to us, and so should we not prevent a massacre? But this might antagonise Tito and provoke Russia. And so on. One could begin to see how the simplicities of war might be easier to deal with than the complexities of peace.

We drove north in our motley convoy by-passing Venice and going through Udine into Austria at Villach. We hardly cared where we would end up; this was the sort of uncertainty to which we had become accustomed. The rumours gathered like dark clouds: Tito might be wanting to grab a chunk of Austria, but if we moved too many troops into Austria he might grab Trieste in Italy. There was a pro-German force somewhere in the hills which consisted of Russian anti-Bolshevik Cossacks who had been fighting for the Germans; they too said they would only surrender to the British because in the hands of anyone else they would be likely to be slaughtered. In the meantime the Irish Brigade had taken over a warehouse containing tens of thousands of bottles of the Austrian liqueur schnapps; so that the political situation assumed an air of less importance. It was even said that someone somewhere had captured a mint which was churning out a stream of paper money. Then a new and mythical-sounding threat was said to be on the horizon – the Bulgarians! But no one seemed quite to know on which side they had been or would be fighting.

The London Irish were sent off (though my memories of this are hazy) to make some sort of contact with the Russians. We made a dash to Wolfsberg in the eastern Austrian Alps; the Russians had got as far as Graz, some thirty miles further. We sent out scouting parties; what on earth were we supposed to do if we came across Russians? Offer them some schnapps? I have a picture in my mind of myself and my platoon arriving in some small-town square and seeing across the road some men in strange uniforms whom we took to be Russians – unsmiling and bulging out of jackets that seemed too small for them. We eyed each other warily. Then probably because none of us understood a word of each other's language we wandered into the middle of the square and nodded and made friends. In *The History of the Irish Brigade* it is recorded that there was a conference held at Wolfsberg in the Officers' Mess of the London Irish Rifles, at which territorial boundaries were agreed between the British and Russian forces. This was facilitated, it is suggested, not so much by schnapps, as by alarm about the intentions of the Bulgarians.

Then after a week in Wolfsberg during which some of all of this must have been sorted out – or must have come to be considered not really necessary to be sorted out – we withdrew to Villach, and then to villages on the northern coast of the Ossiachersee, one of the most beautiful lakes in Carinthia, the Austrian province bordering on the frontier with Italy. And there the London Irish stayed for the rest of my time with them in Austria.

What had struck us all on our entry into Austria was not only the beauty of the place and people but the orderliness, peacefulness, the lack of signs of war. The people were neither overtly friendly nor hostile; they were dignified and courteous, and paid attention to what we required. This was especially striking to the communist Desmond Fay, who on entering a recently Nazi-dominated country had expected – what? A people arrogant and savagely embittered? Desmond could laugh and shake his head about what he in fact found; but it was something that made us all wonder, even if we could not work out exactly what. We were at first billeted in an orphanage for children whose parents had been killed in the war: there were Germans and Poles as well as Austrians. The children all seemed to have pale fair hair and the most beautiful manners as well as looks. The women in charge of them herded them into outlying buildings to make room for us; we found ourselves treating the women as if they were our hostesses and we were their guests. When we first arrived there was an army rule that there should be no fraternisation with local people; later this was relaxed because it was unworkable as well as senseless. There were few men except the old left in the villages; the girls and our young soldiers began to flirt not undecorously.

We eventually had to hand over the cars we had taken as loot. Some officers came to arrangements with local farmers to keep and hide their cars until such a time as they could come and pick them up when they were out of the army.

There was still much to do with the huge number of German soldiers and officials who were keen to give themselves up – for the reason that they wanted to be fed, as well as not to fall into the hands of the Russians. From the crowds of these there had to be weeded out and interrogated those who had been Nazis in positions of responsibility who might now be prosecuted as war criminals. In the early stages of this process I was sometimes called on to act as an interpreter with my primitive German. This attempt was apt to dissolve into farce. But there were other situations that became tragically serious.

The Russian Cossack Corps that had been fighting for the Germans against what they saw as an alien Bolshevik Russia had succeeded in surrendering to the British; many had their families with them; they knew that if they were sent or taken back to Russia they would all almost certainly be shot. The Russians demanded that they should be handed over; the British prevaricated. But there had been an agreement between Churchill, Stalin and Roosevelt at the Yalta Conference earlier in the year that all such prisoners should be returned to the country they originally came from. The Cossacks could claim that they had been turned out of their country by the Bolsheviks and thus they had no country, but this carried no weight with the Russians. Orders came down from London that the Cossacks and their families, who had been camping in fields, were to be put forcibly into railway trucks and handed to the Russians. By good fortune the Irish Brigade were not required to do this. But we heard of it; and worried – What would we have done? There was a story that heartened us of a Commanding Officer of the 6th Armoured Division who went to the assembled Cossacks in their field and told them of the orders he had received, and that as a dutiful soldier he would have to obey them; but he would not do so until morning, and in the meantime he would remove his soldiers who were guarding the field because they were tired. And so in the morning the Cossacks and their families had gone – to mingle presumably with the hordes of displaced and often unidentifiable persons throughout Europe.

There was a similar situation with the Croatians who had been hostile to Tito's partisans and in some cases sided with the Germans. Tito was demanding that they should be handed over to him because he was now de facto ruler of Yugoslavia: but if this happened it was likely that they too would be shot. Tito gave assurances they would be treated according to conventions. They were handed over; but there is evidence that most of them were shot.

Could anything have been done to prevent this? The world of politicians and top military authorities is dependent on words and bits of paper: there have been such and such discussions and agreements; out of the boundless chaos of five years of war such people have to try to produce order. On the ground individuals face a different kind of obligation; one should not be responsible for sending off persons to be needlessly murdered. Perhaps indeed the individual soldiers on the spot have a duty to try to save politicians from the sins of their terrible calling (this was a view voiced at the Nuremberg trials). The politicians may be faced with unavoidable choices of evils; soldiers may have to risk covering for them and suffering the cost.

But, in the vast maelstrom that follows from the crack-up of the ice-floes of war, what can any individual do with certainty, whether soldier or politician? One hopes to do one's best.

At the Ossiachersee I was made Battalion Sports Officer, whose job it was to provide occupation for those who had nothing much more militarily to do. I organised conventional games; I could pick myself for any team I liked. I had never been much good at cricket, but here I could at least show off. Also at hockey, which I had never played before. But at football I had to deselect myself: almost anyone seemed better than me. But I had been a good runner at school, so I entered myself for the 440 yards at the Army Games at Klagenfurt – and came in a long way

behind the champion of the Jewish Brigade who was said to have
run at the White City. After this I thought I should retire from
organised sport. At Ossiachersee I watched with some admiration the flirtation games that one or two of my fellow young
officers played with a very pretty young Austrian nurse at the
orphanage.

It was during these days that in the course of a conversation
with Desmond Fay I let on that I had been to school at Eton. He
had long since come to terms with me being the son of Oswald
Mosley; he had said – Oh well, he was a serious politician. But
at the news that I was an Old Etonian he announced he was so
upset that he was not sure if he could carry on with our friendship. This was not entirely a joke: it is part of Leninist theory
that fascism is not the unequivocal enemy of communism – it
can be a necessary stage in the collapse of capitalism. The clear-
cut enemies of the communist proletariat have always been the
upper classes.

I went on a week's leave to Venice and stayed on the Lido,
where I had stayed with my father and mother in the summer
holidays of 1930. Then my father had spent much time flirting
with my future stepmother Diana, who at that time was married
to Brian Guinness. My sister and I, I remembered, had spent
much time being outraged not at my father's behaviour to my
mother, which I suppose we either did not notice or took as
normal upper-class behaviour, but because Randolph Churchill,
one of my father's and mother's entourage, insisted on referring
to us children as 'brats.' Now, on leave in Venice, I wrote to my
father that I did not want to do any more sight-seeing; I wanted
to come home. In continuation of the letters I had written from

Ranby and Naples, still in pursuit of what now increasingly ob-
sessed me – the question of how to look for what might be an
alternative to human's propensity for war – I wrote –

> I wonder if Neitzsche's final madness was really the
> decadent desperation that people suppose – if it were
> not 'tragic' in the ultimate sense – the culmination
> of a tragedy in the true Greek style – and therefore
> something to be greeted and accepted with a 'holy
> yea-saying'? Is anything much known of Nietzsche's
> final madness? It is a theory that entrances me – that
> it is perhaps the culmination of all 'great spirits' that
> they should appear to be what the rest of the world
> calls mad: that perhaps this one form of madness – the
> Dionysian madness – is really an escape into the 'eter-
> nity behind reality': neither an advance nor a regres-
> sion in life but just a sidestep into something that is
> always beside life. Or am I slightly mad?
>
> It seems to me that the physicists have argued
> themselves out of their original premises and are float-
> ing blindly . . . if all our sense-perceptions, measures,
> observations etc, are unreliable, indeed misleading,
> when it comes to interpreting the 'real' world, why
> do they presume that any experiment they make has
> any bearing on reality at all? The only thing they can
> be certain about is that they can never be certain of
> anything . . .
>
> It seems that the infinite only makes itself known to
> the finite by means of selected symbols or 'emotions'

(which perhaps are only the result of symbol-action):
it is beyond the comprehension of the finite (human?)
mind to understand the reality behind these symbols.
But this does not exclude the possibility of creating
– through a fuller understanding of the symbols – a
higher form of consciousness which might ultimately
glimpse the reality that lies behind.

I had long since seen that my father looked on Nietzsche's
work mainly in political terms, whereas I saw it as dealing with
metaphysics – in that Nietzsche had seen that language was what
humans used in their exercise of power, and that any idea of
'truth' had to recognise this and somehow overcome it. Hence
Nietzsche's extraordinary elliptical, ironic, highly wrought style
that had to be understood by a reader as an artwork rather than
an argument. I hoped to go up to Oxford after I got out of the
army in order to read philosophy and to try to get more straight
my ideas about all this. (But then when I did get to Oxford my
tutor said – We don't do Nietzsche – implying that he had been
a Nazi).

Mervyn had left the London Irish in Austria in order to work
on the staff at Central Mediterranean Headquarters. It seemed
that I might not be in a close working relationship with him
again. I had a letter from him –

The chaps here are nice, but at present they seem
solely interested in their work – not because they like
it, because they seem to have been allowed hardly any
other interests during the war. How terrible. There is

also a large content of 'the affected young man' – not your sort of affectation but a far more transparent species of this sometime delectable trait.

Am READING seriously and furiously. Do you know that we have been living in ignorance (I have anyway) of *decadence* (French) as opposed to honest English decadence. The French sort is far more awful and I must define it to you as soon as I understand it so that we can practice it like mad.

Hope you have opened a branch office of the SDA; you should get many members now. I am having no difficulty in extending it here of course.

P.S. Has your mighty epic (which we planned you would publish at the age of 80 years) taken any less amorphous shape?

For many years I forgot I had planned an epic. But here it now is, rarefied and distilled over a lifetime of not knowing quite in what style to write it.

I had been impatient to get home, not only to my family but also to my old school friends; and now when I got back to the battalion from Venice I learned that this would be possible – under the aegis of an army order that all officers and men under a certain age and with less than a certain time of serving overseas were now eligible to be sent to the far east to continue the war against Japan – with the benefit of a month's leave in England first. So my wish to get home was granted: but rather in the manner of that ghost-story in which a couple are given

three wishes, the first two of which are granted in such a horrific manner that the third has to be that the first two should be
cancelled. However I wrote home –

> The authorities declared I was eligible for Burma by
> just three weeks, and nothing that any kindly C.O. or
> Brigadier out here can do can stop me. But as it hap-
> pened I received the news with something like relief,
> and would not now alter the arrangement even if it
> were possible. I have been growing moribund in Aus-
> tria with the harassing job of organising sports from
> the confines of a stuffy office. Leave, I am sure, will
> miraculously revive me.

I don't know how much this was bravado: it was perhaps a
fatalism I had learned; and there might be a way of going east
with my old clique of friends. So off I went from Austria on the
long and by now familiar journey back through Florence and
Rome to Naples to wait for a boat to take me home, if only
en route to tortuous approaches to Japan. I was sitting with a
few fellow travelling companions on the terrace of the Officers'
Club looking out across the beautiful bay at Vesuvius which was
smoking rather ominously in the distance (it had caused some
consternation by half erupting the previous year: this was August
1945) and I was thinking that after all on no account did I want
to go to fight Japan. Then we read in the local army newspaper
that a bomb had been dropped on Japan that was a new sort of
bomb – something to do with what goes on at the heart of the
matter – and its effects were so horrific that countless thousands

of people had been killed and the Japanese were already talking of surrender. In fact its effects were so unknown and so uncanny that in future large-scale wars might be made impossible. So I thought — Well that's not so bad then! Good old whatever-it-is at the heart of matter!

Humans seem at home in war. They feel lost when among the responsibilities of peace. In war they are told what to do: they accept that they have to 'get on with it.' In peace it seems uncertain what they have to do: they have to discover what the 'it' is to get on with.

I had been keen to get home to be with my family and friends, even if it was only for a month before going out to Burma or wherever. But if the war was really about to be over, then it might be possible that I could be at peace in the Far East with my so-called clique of friends? This clique I had fantasised about in Italy was a sort of alternative family; to be enjoyed if possible in conjunction with both my father's and my sister's establishments. At school my friends and I had been, yes, in our attitudes homosexual; though only in one pairing occasionally practicing. For the most part we were fantasy-gay in style, in conceits. In war this style had had to be carried on mainly by letter. But as part of occupying forces in Burma, Malaysia — might not three or four of us form an exotic home from home?

When I had gone from public school straight into the army this had seemed to be a continuation of a homosexual world in which there were no natural family ties – no responsibilities, no chance of children. In this sense it had been like the Garden of Eden. Would it be possible to create a peaceful Eden?

In the army in Italy I had hardly thought of myself as homosexual: I had scarcely felt myself sexual at all – sex was an itch that war had pushed into the sidelines. Then when I had been in Naples with Anthony (with whom my friendship was strictly platonic) I had written to a third member of the clique who was recovering from D-Day wounds in England –

> Anthony keeps talking paternally of the ultimate necessity of marriage and family-rearing which, he maintains, involves SETTLING DOWN at some quite early date. I do not grant him this last proposition, for I hold that it is just as preferable to be UNSETTLED in marriage as it is out of marriage

And then – 'I WILL NOT BE RESPECTABLE.' And earlier – 'I am both ignorant and disinterested in women.'

But then when I got home to London in September 1945 I found that the whole grandiose social whirl had started up again as if there had been only a blip since September 1939. Almost every night there were what used to be known as debutante dances; to which those thought to be socially acceptable were invited and to which I had the entree through my sister Vivien and my aunt Irene Ravensdale. And each of these dances seemed to consist of an enchanted garden of girls: how was it possible that I had not noticed girls before? Now suddenly they seemed to be everywhere and infinitely alluring; as thick on the ground as – how might it be put – 'autumnal leaves that strow the brooks in Vallombrosa'? But had not this referred to fallen angels? Well so be it. If it was love that one wanted – take one's pick!

But here was a problem: how on earth did one pick and choose? In a heterosexual world it seemed that one was expected to fall in love with just one girl: but surely with such profusion one wanted the whole lot – or at least a big bunch, an armful. But this was held to be not acceptable.

Such were the dilemmas when one was over the edge into peace, I learned that two of my old school friends were settling in to the Far East. But now, surely, it would be more pleasant and even vital for me to stay in London and explore the peace-time possibilities, however baffling, of getting to grips with women.

But with my orders to embark for Malaysia having come through, how would this be possible? After such homosexual affectations, in the heterosexual world had my luck run out?

Then at one of these dances – at the Savoy Hotel I think – I had retired to the bar in some exhaustion from trying to squeeze what dalliance I could into what time I had left, and there I came across a Major whom I knew slightly, or perhaps he was a friend of my sister's; and he asked me what I was doing nowadays; and I said I was just off to the Far East. And he said – My dear fellow, why on earth do you want to do that? And I said – I don't. So he said – Come and see me in the War Office in the morning. So I did: and I did not know if he would even remember me. But there he was, behind a desk even if somewhat holding his head;

and he said – I'm afraid I can't quite manage the War Office, but would a job in Eastern Command, Hounslow, do? And I said – Indeed, thank you, Eastern Command, Hounslow, would do very well. So in a day or two I received papers taking me off the draft to the Far East and instructing me to report to Hounslow Barracks – a gaunt building like a furniture depository some ten miles west of London. There no one was expecting me; but I was given a desk and a chair where I sat and wondered once more in what style I would one day be able to try to write about war – its luck that seemed to take the place of conventional responsibility. At intervals I played ping-pong with the man with whom I shared an office, using our desks pushed together as a table and copies of *The Manual of Military Law* as bats. Eventually work was found for me which was to do with officers' pay and courts martial – the latter often dealing with officers caught and photographed as transvestites. And in the evening I would catch the District Line back to London where I continued to learn the pleasure of prowling in search of – yes this was surely a better way of putting it – the rose among the rosebud garden of girls.

So this was peace? But there remained the problem of how to make sense of responsibility.

When people said at the end of the war that they found themselves at a loss – they could no longer feel that they just had to 'get on with it' but now had to find the 'it' that they had to get on with – was this 'it' really just the evolutionary business of finding a mate, settling down, procreation? But humans had always found confusion with this; was it not a sort of war? But in so-called 'peace' there were no longer orders coming down from on high; or if religion or social custom claimed that there were, then it was still up to the judgment of individuals to respect these or reject them. Humans had to make their own dispositions to deal with the 'its' that they were finding they had to get on with – work, faith, relationships. And regarding these they felt not only at a loss, but that such a feeling was somehow reprehensible – for should not at least love, the commitment to love, the care of children (so they had an instinct to believe) be sweetness and light? And if it was not, should there really be only themselves to blame? Humans were thrown into the deep end of peace and had to learn how to swim. But why had it ever been thought that peace should be easy? If peace involved the requirement to take responsibility for oneself – then all right, yes, it could be seen how obedience in war might be easier.

I remained in the army working at Hounslow for another year. During this time I did not in fact feel that I had much responsibility. It was still ordained that I should travel on the Underground out and back each day. In the evenings amongst those with whom I behaved irresponsibly it could be accepted that I was still involved in some hangover from the war.

At weekends I would go to stay with my father who was now out of politics as well as house arrest and was leading the life of a country gentleman in Wiltshire. When I had first arrived home, landing off the troop-ship at Liverpool, I had gone straight to my sister Vivien who was still with her friends Rosalind and Rosie in a flat off Knightsbridge: then late that night we had driven down to my father and Diana who were waiting up to welcome me with cups of tea and snacks. There was so much that might be talked about that I at least could hardly talk at all; I wondered if

I would ever be able to talk about the war. This was my family, and had been my home; but it did not seem, however my war ended, that I would be able to settle here again.

When I was working in Hounslow and went to stay with my father at weekends, we chatted easily enough about our shared philosophical and literary interests; but our conversation did not have the same intensity as our letters had had in war. I remained perhaps closer to my sister Vivien, who set up her own establishment in the country with our brother Micky and our old Nanny. When Mervyn Davies came home shortly after me, I introduced him to Vivien and I hoped they might form some relationship; but I suppose inevitably nothing came of this. When Mervyn got out of the army he resumed his studies in law; he became a QC, and later a High Court Judge. We still see each other at intervals to have lunch.

My friends in the Far East wrote that they were having a fine time running a local radio station through which they could broadcast their poetry. And they were sharing a mistress. Affectations of homosexuality seemed to be being blown away by peace.

I discovered that there was a way by which I could get out of the army earlier than I had expected. Shortly before I had joined up in 1942 I had taken a scholarship exam for Balliol College, Oxford; I had done little work for this knowing that I would be going off to war. But Balliol had said I had done well enough for them to keep a place for me if later I wanted it. And now it seemed that if I chose to take up this offer I could be demobilised by October 1946 rather than almost a year later. This I did. I wanted to read philosophy – to continue in a more disciplined manner my efforts to understand, amongst other things, why humans seemed to be at home in war, but to refuse to acknowledge this and thus to be able to deal with it.

Then when I got to Oxford I was told that this was not what philosophy was about. The ancient Greek tragedians, yes, had been interested in such questions, but they came under the heading of Classics. The Existentialists? Nietzsche? They did not 'do' these at Oxford. What did they do? Descartes, Hume, Kant: Epistemology, the Theory of Knowledge: what do we mean when we say that we 'know.' But was not this what Nietzsche was on about? Was it? But I had always felt that I would have to work things out for myself.

I stayed at Oxford for just the year I would otherwise have been in the army. Then I left to write my first novel. If academic study insisted on dealing with only the bones of theory, then surely it was up to novels to portray the flesh of life. Also I left Oxford to marry Rosemary, my eventually chosen rose from the rosebud garden of girls.

I had first noticed Rosemary at one of the innumerable fashionable dances in London. It seemed she had noticed me. But we had been wary: if one pounced conventionally, surely any quarry worth catching would have to try to get away? So how in fact, when it came to it, *did* one pick and choose? One waited for some sign, some singularity; some jungle-test like that of a smell?

I bumped into Rosemary again some months later in a coffee-bar in Oxford. I said 'Do you remember me?' She said 'Yes.' I said 'Good.' She said 'I thought you were that murderer.' There was a murderer on the loose at the time who was said to chop up women and dissolve them in the bath. I thought – Well this indeed is a singular signal that one cannot precisely explain; but could it fit into a novel?

I took her out to dinner. She hardly spoke. I rattled on. After a time I said 'What are you thinking?' She said 'That I could send you mad in a fortnight.' I said 'Why wait a fortnight?' I went out to where my car was parked and I gave her the keys. I lay down in the road where she could run over me. She said she did not know how to drive. I got up to show her. Then we drove back to her lodging. By the end of the evening I think we both thought we might marry.

The next weekend I suggested we go in my car for a drive in the country. She asked if we could visit her old grandmother who lived in Hertfordshire. I said – Of course. I had the impression that Rosemary's family must be hard up, for in spite of her presence at London dances she appeared to have no money for bus fares and to possess no smart clothes. On Sunday we dove through country lanes and eventually came to the gates and lodge of a drive leading to what must be a large country house. An old lady came out from the lodge to open the gates: I wondered – This is her grandmother? The old lady waved us through. We drove through what seemed to be endless acres of parkland and came to a long low house like a battleship. We went in through a back door and along stone passages where all life seemed to have stopped; then through a baize door to a small sitting room outside which Rosemary asked me to wait for a moment. Then when I went in there was a very old lady in a wheel chair who, when her granddaughter had introduced me, said 'And I was such a friend of your grandfather's!'

I still had no idea who this lady could be who had been a friend of my grandfather Lord Curzon. (I managed a bit later to glimpse an envelope lying on a desk addressed to 'Lady Desborough.') She asked Rosemary if I would like to see what she referred to as 'the paintings.' She gave Rosemary a huge old-fashioned key and we went down a central corridor of tattered grandeur and into a long high picture gallery where, when Rosemary had opened a creaking shutter, there appeared – through cobwebs – a Van Dyke? An Italian renaissance Holy Family? A huge portrait of a soldier on a horse that could be – surely not! – a Rembrandt? (Rosemary said – Yes, they say it is.) I thought it important that I should not appear to be bowled over by all this. Why should it not be as natural as anything else? But it seemed more likely than ever that we would marry.

*   *   *

So this was peace. But there still seems to me, sixty years later, to be a problem of how to write about war. From the complexities of peace you can produce an artwork. From the simplicities of war – can you portray in one breath both heroism and horror?

People are not supposed to write about their successful exploits in war: this is considered to be bad form. And about the exploits of others – well, this is easier to write when they are dead. There is a whiff of immature triumphalism in stories about successful killing – unless one has paid the price of being killed oneself. Good stories were able to be written about the First World War because then the whole absurdity could be seen as just horror, a senseless disaster. But the Second World War had not been like this — had it? It was held to be just and right. And yet there were the horrors, the disasters. There are very few good stories about the fighting in the Second World War — one of them, as I have mentioned, is Raleigh Trevelyan's *The Fortress*, about the landing at Anzio. A good story about the Second World War has to comprise a way of writing about the horror and the rightness, the misery and the satisfaction, the evil and the good, all in one. Not a problem for epistemology? No?

Perhaps more a problem for religion. The old Greeks had gods — and so did Nietzsche, although he exclaimed that his god was dead. (I later suggested in a novel that such a god might better be seen as a successful train-robber retired to the Argentine). Anyway, not much of a task here, it is true, for logical or verifiable thinking. But then what should be the style? What about my own candidate for Good Fairy — that which goes on at the heart of matter? Here, one is told, things can both be and not be at the same time; an observer affects that which is observed; reality is a function of the experimental condition. So indeed, why should not this be the style in which one might float in the deep end of peace? A lifetime's effort indeed! Or would one rather drown?

Humans seem at home in war: they do not feel at home in peace. This cannot often enough be said. So long as it is denied — so long as it is thought that peace is prevented by the actions of certain misfits — then humans cannot learn. There are few novels written about how to live in peace; they are held to be boring. People prefer to read about, and indeed many to experience, the senseless excitement of the simulation of war; the dicing with destruction and the risk of being dead. But if this is the condition on which evolution has depended and which has brought us to where we are, then it hardly makes sense to object – unless, that is, it is seen that evolution has also brought us to an awareness that this condition has become too dangerous and might be surmounted: one can be conscious, that is, of existence on another level.

Evolution had depended on carnage: some species have to be destroyed so that others survive. On the way however there have also evolved alliances, dependences, symbioses, by which some species may help each other to survive, even if at the cost of others. It seems that humans have evolved an ability to be aware of this, even if they do not seem able to stop being at war within and amongst themselves. They see they have their animal nature; and somewhat at odds with this their human nature which sees the possibility of something different; but they do not seem to have evolved a strategy by which to be at ease with this – except perhaps through the creation and recognition of works of art. In the course of evolution, that is, they have experienced an order beyond that of animal or even human nature – an order which seems to be outside evolution because it sees how evolution can be assessed and even reorganised. This order seems to manifest itself as infinite, eternal: humans have called it the supernatural or spiritual; and it can naturally, of course, be said not to exist. But it seems to have arisen from a tendency of humans to try to make sense of their situation – that of being confined in an evolutionary process and yet also experiencing that a part of them is free of this and even at times can influence it. They may attempt this by art; or perhaps do it best by seeing their situation as funny.

Even in formal war there had seemed to be some spiritual ordering as well as orders coming down through chains of command: how else did I stay alive? You get on with things as best you can: but then what does 'best' involve? You keep your eyes and ears open; you learn the limitations of orders; you become aware of an ability within yourself to know what further is required. And then, when necessary, you are ready to jump in at a deep end. But I have told my story.

My last letter to my friend Timmy before he went out to Burma still hoping, perhaps, to 'prove' himself in war, was –

> I feel that you were right in your decision to issue Burmawards. Not, however for the reason you give. Life in battle is the most futile thing in the world, for it is the only futility about which one is forced to care desperately. And for this reason it is the most unreal thing in the world. Indeed its most potent effect upon me was to suggest that there was no reality in anything; that all was the wild imagination of an aimless mind. I now think nothing: I am too weary to wonder about the unreality of reality: I have reached the stage where everything must be accepted or rejected without inquiry. All that I have learnt of men is that they are composed of such a mixture of perfidy and nobility as I cannot hope to unravel; and all I have learnt of life is that there is nothing more to be known about it save that which is observable at the end of one's nose.

But then I had come home – to the garden of fallen angels: to the chance of a lifetime's learning about the paradoxes of peace?

Rosemary and I married: we got away from our families for a time by going to live on a small hill farm in north Wales – me to run the farm and to write my first novel; Rosemary to paint. Writers and painters should have one foot on the earth, should they not, as well as their heads in the clouds? But then children arrived; and we had no piped water, and in winter the stream that ran past the house froze, and roads became blocked: so after a few years Rosemary's mother suggested that for our family's sake she should hand over to us her commodious house in Sussex which was now too big for her; and this seemed an offer we could not refuse. This story and others that follow I have told in my autobiography *Efforts at Truth.*

My friend Anthony, after a year or two in the wilderness of peace, announced that he was intending to become an Anglican monk. Then a few years later my other great friend, Timmy, went to train to be a priest; and I myself was struggling to learn to be a Christian. All this was a consequence of our coming across, in turn, a holy man, Father Raynes (I have told this story more than once): but it was also, it seems to me now, of our having, in our formative years, put everything up to question even if in our fanciful style; of our having treated nothing as sacrosanct except that one should be ready, when the time seems to have come, to jump in at a deep end. We needed for a time to put our trust in orders that might seem to be come from above; then later I at least (and this was what I became convinced Christ and Christianity were saying) believed that whatever was necessary could be known less through commands from outside than from a faculty for ordering that had grown within oneself.

About my relationship with my father – I remained on good terms with him so long as he remained a gentleman farmer. But by 1948 he was being enticed back into politics and I did not see so much of him; and anyway Rosemary and I had married and were escaping to North Wales. Then at the end of the 1950s he was standing as a parliamentary candidate for North Kensington hoping apparently to attract the anti-black vote; and I became determined to have a decisive emotional confrontation with him. I managed this; and in the course of it he said he would never speak to me again. This situation lasted for several years. Then at the end of his life when he had Parkinson's disease and was finally out of politics I became close to him again. He was as he had been in prison – resigned and benign and trying to look back on what had gone wrong and what might have gone right. We talked in our old free-wheeling style; and just a week before he died he announced that he wished me to have all his papers so that I could write about him. He knew how much I had disapproved of his politics: he also knew I would try to tell the truth as I saw it because that had been our style.

About my loves – my marriages to my first wife Rosemary and to my second wife Verity – I have tried to tell of these in my novels. The style is one which tries to portray the hope of peace but the near impossibility of achieving it; a condition in which there seems to be no orders but only paradoxical demands for self-ordering. Love has to be self-giving yet you have to make of yourself something to give: marriage should purvey not only possession but autonomy. This is what seems impossible: but also what, if admitted, seems possible though grace. Peace can be found in the mind and in the heart. War, evolution, can go on elsewhere.

SELECTED DALKEY ARCHIVE PAPERBACKS

PETROS ABATZOGLOU, *What Does Mrs. Freeman Want?*
PIERRE ALBERT-BIROT, *Grabinoulor.*
YUZ ALESHKOVSKY, *Kangaroo.*
FELIPE ALFAU, *Chromos.*
  Locos.
IVAN ÂNGELO, *The Celebration.*
  The Tower of Glass.
DAVID ANTIN, *Talking.*
DJUNA BARNES, *Ladies Almanack.*
  Ryder.
JOHN BARTH, *LETTERS.*
  Sabbatical.
DONALD BARTHELME, *The King.*
  Paradise.
SVETISLAV BASARA, *Chinese Letter.*
MARK BINELLI, *Sacco and Vanzetti Must Die!*
ANDREI BITOV, *Pushkin House.*
LOUIS PAUL BOON, *Chapel Road.*
  Summer in Termuren.
ROGER BOYLAN, *Killoyle.*
IGNÁCIO DE LOYOLA BRANDÃO, *Teeth under the Sun.*
  Zero.
CHRISTINE BROOKE-ROSE, *Amalgamemnon.*
BRIGID BROPHY, *In Transit.*
MEREDITH BROSNAN, *Mr. Dynamite.*
GERALD L. BRUNS,
  Modern Poetry and the Idea of Language.
GABRIELLE BURTON, *Heartbreak Hotel.*
MICHEL BUTOR, *Degrees.*
  Mobile.
  Portrait of the Artist as a Young Ape.
G. CABRERA INFANTE, *Infante's Inferno.*
  Three Trapped Tigers.
JULIETA CAMPOS, *The Fear of Losing Eurydice.*
ANNE CARSON, *Eros the Bittersweet.*
CAMILO JOSÉ CELA, *The Family of Pascual Duarte.*
  The Hive.
LOUIS-FERDINAND CÉLINE, *Castle to Castle.*
  Conversations with Professor Y.
  London Bridge.
  North.
  Rigadoon.
HUGO CHARTERIS, *The Tide Is Right.*
JEROME CHARYN, *The Tar Baby.*
MARC CHOLODENKO, *Mordechai Schamz.*
EMILY HOLMES COLEMAN, *The Shutter of Snow.*
ROBERT COOVER, *A Night at the Movies.*
STANLEY CRAWFORD, *Some Instructions to My Wife.*
ROBERT CREELEY, *Collected Prose.*
RENÉ CREVEL, *Putting My Foot in It.*
RALPH CUSACK, *Cadenza.*
SUSAN DAITCH, *L.C.*
  Storytown.
NIGEL DENNIS, *Cards of Identity.*
PETER DIMOCK,
  A Short Rhetoric for Leaving the Family.
ARIEL DORFMAN, *Konfidenz.*
COLEMAN DOWELL, *The Houses of Children.*
  Island People.
  Too Much Flesh and Jabez.
RIKKI DUCORNET, *The Complete Butcher's Tales.*
  The Fountains of Neptune.
  The Jade Cabinet.
  Phosphor in Dreamland.
  The Stain.
  The Word "Desire."
WILLIAM EASTLAKE, *The Bamboo Bed.*
  Castle Keep.
  Lyric of the Circle Heart.
JEAN ECHENOZ, *Chopin's Move.*
STANLEY ELKIN, *A Bad Man.*
  Boswell: A Modern Comedy.
  Criers and Kibitzers, Kibitzers and Criers.
  The Dick Gibson Show.
  The Franchiser.
  George Mills.
  The Living End.
  The MacGuffin.
  The Magic Kingdom.
  Mrs. Ted Bliss.
  The Rabbi of Lud.

  Van Gogh's Room at Arles.
ANNIE ERNAUX, *Cleaned Out.*
LAUREN FAIRBANKS, *Muzzle Thyself.*
  Sister Carrie.
LESLIE A. FIEDLER,
  Love and Death in the American Novel.
GUSTAVE FLAUBERT, *Bouvard and Pécuchet.*
FORD MADOX FORD, *The March of Literature.*
JON FOSSE, *Melancholy.*
MAX FRISCH, *I'm Not Stiller.*
CARLOS FUENTES, *Christopher Unborn.*
  Distant Relations.
  Terra Nostra.
  Where the Air Is Clear.
JANICE GALLOWAY, *Foreign Parts.*
  The Trick Is to Keep Breathing.
WILLIAM H. GASS, *The Tunnel.*
  Willie Masters' Lonesome Wife.
ETIENNE GILSON, *The Arts of the Beautiful.*
  Forms and Substances in the Arts.
C. S. GISCOMBE, *Giscome Road.*
  Here.
DOUGLAS GLOVER, *Bad News of the Heart.*
  The Enamoured Knight.
KAREN ELIZABETH GORDON, *The Red Shoes.*
GEORGI GOSPODINOV, *Natural Novel.*
JUAN GOYTISOLO, *Marks of Identity.*
PATRICK GRAINVILLE, *The Cave of Heaven.*
HENRY GREEN, *Blindness.*
  Concluding.
  Doting.
  Nothing.
JIŘÍ GRUŠA, *The Questionnaire.*
JOHN HAWKES, *Whistlejacket.*
AIDAN HIGGINS, *A Bestiary.*
  Bornholm Night-Ferry.
  Flotsam and Jetsam.
  Langrishe, Go Down.
  Scenes from a Receding Past.
  Windy Arbours.
ALDOUS HUXLEY, *Antic Hay.*
  Crome Yellow.
  Point Counter Point.
  Those Barren Leaves.
  Time Must Have a Stop.
MIKHAIL IOSSEL AND JEFF PARKER, EDS., *Amerika:*
  Contemporary Russians View
  the United States.
GERT JONKE, *Geometric Regional Novel.*
JACQUES JOUET, *Mountain R.*
HUGH KENNER, *The Counterfeiters.*
  Flaubert, Joyce and Beckett:
  The Stoic Comedians.
  Joyce's Voices.
DANILO KIŠ, *Garden, Ashes.*
  A Tomb for Boris Davidovich.
ANITA KONKKA, *A Fool's Paradise.*
TADEUSZ KONWICKI, *A Minor Apocalypse.*
  The Polish Complex.
MENIS KOUMANDAREAS, *Koula.*
ELAINE KRAF, *The Princess of 72nd Street.*
JIM KRUSOE, *Iceland.*
EWA KURYLUK, *Century 21.*
VIOLETTE LEDUC, *La Bâtarde.*
DEBORAH LEVY, *Billy and Girl.*
  Pillow Talk in Europe and Other Places.
JOSÉ LEZAMA LIMA, *Paradiso.*
ROSA LIKSOM, *Dark Paradise.*
OSMAN LINS, *Avalovara.*
  The Queen of the Prisons of Greece.
ALF MAC LOCHLAINN, *The Corpus in the Library.*
  Out of Focus.
RON LOEWINSOHN, *Magnetic Field(s).*
D. KEITH MANO, *Take Five.*
BEN MARCUS, *The Age of Wire and String.*
WALLACE MARKFIELD, *Teitlebaum's Window.*
  To an Early Grave.
DAVID MARKSON, *Reader's Block.*
  Springer's Progress.
  Wittgenstein's Mistress.

FOR A FULL LIST OF PUBLICATIONS, VISIT:
www.dalkeyarchive.com

SELECTED DALKEY ARCHIVE PAPERBACKS

CAROLE MASO, *AVA*.

LADISLAV MATEJKA AND KRYSTYNA POMORSKA, EDS.,
Readings in Russian Poetics: Formalist and Structuralist Views.

HARRY MATHEWS,
The Case of the Persevering Maltese: Collected Essays.
Cigarettes.
The Conversions.
The Human Country: New and Collected Stories.
The Journalist.
My Life in CIA.
Singular Pleasures.
The Sinking of the Odradek Stadium.
Tlooth.
20 Lines a Day.

ROBERT L. MCLAUGHLIN, ED.,
Innovations: An Anthology of Modern & Contemporary Fiction.

HERMAN MELVILLE, *The Confidence-Man*.

STEVEN MILLHAUSER, *The Barnum Museum*.
In the Penny Arcade.

RALPH J. MILLS, JR., *Essays on Poetry*.

OLIVE MOORE, *Spleen*.

NICHOLAS MOSLEY, *Accident*.
Assassins.
Catastrophe Practice.
Children of Darkness and Light.
Experience and Religion.
The Hesperides Tree.
Hopeful Monsters.
Imago Bird.
Impossible Object.
Inventing God.
Judith.
Look at the Dark.
Natalie Natalia.
Serpent.
Time at War.
The Uses of Slime Mould: Essays of Four Decades.

WARREN F. MOTTE, JR.,
Fables of the Novel: French Fiction since 1990.
Oulipo: A Primer of Potential Literature.

YVES NAVARRE, *Our Share of Time*.
Sweet Tooth.

DOROTHY NELSON, *In Night's City*.
Tar and Feathers.

WILFRIDO D. NOLLEDO, *But for the Lovers*.

FLANN O'BRIEN, *At Swim-Two-Birds*.
At War.
The Best of Myles.
The Dalkey Archive.
Further Cuttings.
The Hard Life.
The Poor Mouth.
The Third Policeman.

CLAUDE OLLIER, *The Mise-en-Scène*.

PATRIK OUŘEDNÍK, *Europeana*.

FERNANDO DEL PASO, *Palinuro of Mexico*.

ROBERT PINGET, *The Inquisitory*.
Mahu or The Material.
Trio.

RAYMOND QUENEAU, *The Last Days*.
Odile.
Pierrot Mon Ami.
Saint Glinglin.

ANN QUIN, *Berg*.
Passages.
Three.
Tripticks.

ISHMAEL REED, *The Free-Lance Pallbearers*.
The Last Days of Louisiana Red.
Reckless Eyeballing.
The Terrible Threes.
The Terrible Twos.
Yellow Back Radio Broke-Down.

JULIÁN RÍOS, *Larva: A Midsummer Night's Babel*.
Poundemonium.

AUGUSTO ROA BASTOS, *I the Supreme*.

JACQUES ROUBAUD, *The Great Fire of London*.
Hortense in Exile.

Hortense Is Abducted.
The Plurality of Worlds of Lewis.
The Princess Hoppy.
The Form of a City Changes Faster, Alas, Than the Human Heart.
Some Thing Black.

LEON S. ROUDIEZ, *French Fiction Revisited*.

VEDRANA RUDAN, *Night*.

LYDIE SALVAYRE, *The Company of Ghosts*.
Everyday Life.
The Lecture.

LUIS RAFAEL SÁNCHEZ, *Macho Camacho's Beat*.

SEVERO SARDUY, *Cobra & Maitreya*.

NATHALIE SARRAUTE, *Do You Hear Them?*
Martereau.
The Planetarium.

ARNO SCHMIDT, *Collected Stories*.
Nobodaddy's Children.

CHRISTINE SCHUTT, *Nightwork*.

GAIL SCOTT, *My Paris*.

JUNE AKERS SEESE,
Is This What Other Women Feel Too?
What Waiting Really Means.

AURELIE SHEEHAN, *Jack Kerouac Is Pregnant*.

VIKTOR SHKLOVSKY, *Knight's Move*.
A Sentimental Journey: Memoirs 1917-1922.
Theory of Prose.
Third Factory.
Zoo, or Letters Not about Love.

JOSEF ŠKVORECKÝ,
The Engineer of Human Souls.

CLAUDE SIMON, *The Invitation*.

GILBERT SORRENTINO, *Aberration of Starlight*.
Blue Pastoral.
Crystal Vision.
Imaginative Qualities of Actual Things.
Mulligan Stew.
Pack of Lies.
Red the Fiend.
The Sky Changes.
Something Said.
Splendide-Hôtel.
Steelwork.
Under the Shadow.

W. M. SPACKMAN, *The Complete Fiction*.

GERTRUDE STEIN, *Lucy Church Amiably*.
The Making of Americans.
A Novel of Thank You.

PIOTR SZEWC, *Annihilation*.

STEFAN THEMERSON, *Hobson's Island*.
The Mystery of the Sardine.
Tom Harris.

JEAN-PHILIPPE TOUSSAINT, *Television*.

DUMITRU TSEPENEAG, *Vain Art of the Fugue*.

ESTHER TUSQUETS, *Stranded*.

DUBRAVKA UGRESIC, *Lend Me Your Character*.
Thank You for Not Reading.

MATI UNT, *Things in the Night*.

ELOY URROZ, *The Obstacles*.

LUISA VALENZUELA, *He Who Searches*.

BORIS VIAN, *Heartsnatcher*.

PAUL WEST, *Words for a Deaf Daughter & Gala*.

CURTIS WHITE, *America's Magic Mountain*.
The Idea of Home.
Memories of My Father Watching TV.
Monstrous Possibility: An Invitation to Literary Politics.
Requiem.

DIANE WILLIAMS, *Excitability: Selected Stories*.
Romancer Erector.

DOUGLAS WOOLF, *Wall to Wall*.
Ya! & John-Juan.

PHILIP WYLIE, *Generation of Vipers*.

MARGUERITE YOUNG, *Angel in the Forest*.
Miss MacIntosh, My Darling.

REYOUNG, *Unbabbling*.

ZORAN ŽIVKOVIĆ, *Hidden Camera*.

LOUIS ZUKOFSKY, *Collected Fiction*.

SCOTT ZWIREN, *God Head*.

FOR A FULL LIST OF PUBLICATIONS, VISIT:

www.dalkeyarchive.com